PARANORMAL
CHELTENHAM

PARANORMAL CHELTENHAM

ROSS ANDREWS

AMBERLEY

First published 2009

Amberley Publishing Plc
Cirencester Road, Chalford,
Stroud, Gloucestershire, GL6 8PE

www.amberley-books.com

Copyright © Ross Andrews 2009

The right of Ross Andrews to be identified as the Author
of this work has been asserted in accordance with the
Copyrights, Designs and Patents Act 1988.

ISBN 978 1 84868 630 4

British Library Cataloguing in Publication Data.
A catalogue record for this book is available from the
British Library.

Typeset in 10pt on 12pt Sabon.
Typesetting and Origination by FONTHILLDESIGN.
Printed in the UK.

CONTENTS

INTRODUCTION

I am here writing in a cold, dark, candlelit room in a twelfth-century castle that is possibly the most haunted building in all of the United Kingdom. Whilst I am sitting *here*, I am fully aware that, somewhere out *there* in the world is a rather frightened and bewildered person, a person petrified because they are staring at an image floating at the end of their bed. Later, this person will be visited by three more images, each one bringing forth some echo of times gone by or things yet to be — no, wait, I'm getting confused here, that is the plot of *A Christmas Carol* by Charles Dickens.

There is something rather significant about the fact that virtually everyone reading this book will be aware of that great Christmas ghost story. We have a fantastic cultural awareness of what a ghost is, yet when asked 'do you believe in ghosts?', we are all scared to say 'yes' in case we are mocked and pilloried by our peers.

I, however, am perfectly willing to stand up and say, 'I believe in ghosts.' Now, here we have a problem. I usually, at this point, get people sneering and laughing. People comment about how deluded I am and say that I need my head examined. All of the last sentence is probably correct, but, without getting into an existentialist argument as to whether *I* really exist, let us accept that I am not clinically insane. Now, for those of you who know me, that may be a difficult task.

When I say 'I believe in ghosts', what I mean is that you cannot claim that ghosts do not exist, as people see them every day — thousands of people all over the world. At least one in five people claim to have seen what they say is a ghost. What you can say, however, is, 'I am not sure what a ghost is.'

Informed ignorance is my stance in the world of ghost hunting, and anyone who claims that they know what a ghost is, that they can communicate with your dead Auntie Freda or that they can give you the answers to life, the universe and everything is deluded (or they are the spirit of the fantastic, departed author, Douglas Adams, who will tell you it's forty-two).

With the best will in the world, none of these people have all the answers. They may think they have, but any rational scientist will tell you that the best thing about science is that it does not know all the answers. Dara O'Brien, the comedian, once said, 'Science knows it doesn't know all the answers or it would just stop.' However, there are some great advances in the world of quantum physics and chaos theory that could go towards explaining some very interesting paranormal instances and occurrences.

Scientists are only just coming to grips with the 'observer principle'. Now, the paranormal world has known of this for years and called it the 'Laboratory Effect', and it is where molecules behave differently if observed than if not, so at a very basic level it is a form of telekinesis (the movement of matter by paranormal means, normally thought of as the mind moving objects). Now, I could go on and on about paranormal science, and I am sure throughout the book I will give many an example, but I do not wish you to get too steeped in the history or technical aspects of paranormal science.

No. This shall instead be a book about what I do and where I do it, which is, to put it bluntly, ghost busting in Cheltenham and the surrounding areas. I will try and tell you the well-known tales, the not-so-well-known tales and the history of the buildings and town that you are exploring. Obviously, I am reporting not just on the cases I have investigated but also on some of the more famous tales from Cheltenham. It is probable, therefore, that some of these can be found in other publications of Gloucestershire haunting, so whenever possible, I have tried to go back and find out more information, update these stories and check their authenticity.

Now, I have a problem: why should you be interested in the ghosts of Cheltenham and its surrounding locale? There are many answers that I predict will come forth to this question. The first being that possibly you are a tourist and currently standing in the tourist information office trying to find something interesting to do; well, I hope this book can help, as I have written it with Cheltenham ghost walks in mind. I will start you in one place, and tell you about ghost stories as I guide you on short walks throughout this beautiful and scary town. Another reason might be that you are desperately trying to sell your house and are buying this book to find out if it's haunted. Perhaps you even hope that it is haunted and then you can try and claim a twelfth-century headless horseman as some kind of special feature — patio, pond, pebble dashing and phantom. Another reason for buying this book is that you have a wobbly table and this book is just the right thickness to stop the problem when shoved under the leg. Whatever the reason you have for buying this book, my bank manager and I thank you from the heart of my bottom — or even the bottom of my heart.

What I can promise is that it will hopefully be entertaining, informative, fun and also a little bit scary. I can also promise that the stories and events that occur in this book are, to the best of my knowledge, all true. Any experiences I have related from members of PARASOC are also all true. We have no reason to lie; we have always been a non-profit-making organisation with nothing to prove and no belief agenda to preach.

Obviously, when I talk about stories that have happened to other people, you can only take their word for it that they happened the way that they have said. We (PARASOC) will have endeavoured to discover the truth when interviewing all our paranormal witnesses and to find out why they are telling us a story. We are fully aware that people sometimes lie to get publicity for themselves or their premises, and we know that people are sometimes deluded. Our team has several members who work within the mental-health world, so we know that people sometimes just want attention. We have spent a few evenings in supposedly haunted houses with people who really just needed someone to talk to. We have also investigated many houses that turn out to have bad insulation and squeaky floorboards. We have investigated some all because the owner had a faulty digital camera that took some strange pictures, and we have investigated one where, after a Ouija board, someone was convinced the devil lived in their bread bin. I know

I live in a strange world of strange people and strange happenings, so join me, and be strange, in my investigations into the paranormal.

N.B. There are many cases I, along with my team, PARASOC, have investigated throughout Cheltenham and Gloucestershire that I cannot report on for confidentiality reasons. Throughout the book, you will notice that I often mention a building on a certain road rather than the address, this is done so that the present occupiers are not bothered by people knocking on their doors asking questions. Please be aware when on the ghost walks that not all people like the thought of people wandering around looking for phantoms, and for some people, it offends their religious beliefs.

The author

ABOUT THE AUTHOR

Don't panic. I am not going to write a massive autobiography, although it may make sense to tell you about what I do and why I believe in ghosts.

Why I believe is extremely easy to explain: I have seen many ghosts and experienced paranormal activity all my life. What I do is a lot harder to explain, as, technically, I am an entertainer. I sing and perform all over the world, doing cabaret, writing jokes for people and trying to make them laugh and transport them to an escapist world of entertainment. This is not a great starting point for someone who would like to be taken seriously as a paranormal scientist, but I have to put these things in here, as I know full well that sceptical people will read this book and start prying into my history in order to denounce everything I say as pure entertainment, not fact. Obviously, there is nothing I can do to prove to you that what I say is true and that you should believe me just because I say so.

So how do I convince you all of ghosts? The simple answer is that I can't. What I can do is use my position as the chairman of a local paranormal group to tell you the amazing things we have seen and experienced. Now, I do not expect or want you to believe me, but as a scientist, I want you to take what I have said and think about it for yourselves. I will, throughout the course of this book, tell you of the experiments that we (PARASOC) have devised, and I hope you give them all a go. You may wish to find some of the venues that we have been to and see if you can experience any of these hauntings yourselves. More importantly, your house may be haunted and you may want us to come and try to observe your home-grown ghostie.

Now, for the last twenty years of my life, I have been in some fantastic situations, able to observe hauntings, poltergeist activity and general paranormal happenings. I have performed ghost-hunting vigils in some of the world's most haunted buildings and been lucky enough to travel the country, as well as abroad, to investigate these phenomena. However, Gloucestershire always drags me back home because of its fantastic haunted nature and history.

So let's get on with the show. Let me tell you about a very interesting case, which will be the start of our first ghost walk. To make it easier for our visitors to Cheltenham, let's start off in a place that is easy to find. Just off the Promenade we come across the town hall.

Carrie's (aged eight) idea of how the author looks when ghost hunting!

A BRIEF HISTORY OF TIME (OR TOWN)

Early Cheltenham

Cheltenham began its life as a small Saxon village, with a population of a few people and some pigs. At the time of the Domesday Book (1086), it was a small village with a population of less than 200 — I am not sure how many pigs.

However, Cheltenham very soon became a focal point for the surrounding villages. It was because of this that in 1226, King Henry III gave the people of Cheltenham the right to hold a weekly market and an annual fair, where goods were traded, candy floss was eaten, rides on the dodgems were partaken of and pockets were picked (maybe I am zooming forwards a few hundred years?).

Throughout this, Cheltenham remained an agricultural settlement and still a very small town. Most of the people lived by farming. Furthermore, Cheltenham really only had a population of several hundred people right into the Middle Ages. Why we had several hundred middle-aged people I don't know; surely there were some young and old as well. Speaking of very old, one of the only medieval structures to have anything still in place is St Mary's church, which is right in the heart of the town and well worth a visit.

By the seventeenth century, it had grown a little larger and may have had a population of about 1,500. Around this period, there was malting and brewing industry in Cheltenham. There was also a small leather industry and tanners, shoemakers and glovers.

Cheltenham is a famous centre for pre-university learning, with the boys' and ladies' colleges. Perhaps it all started in 1578 when a grammar school was opened.

Cheltenham was changed forever in the early eighteenth century because of water, not like the recent flooding that we have sustained, but salty water. When local people noticed pigeons pecking at salt deposits by a spring south of the town, people began to drink the water believing it would heal all kinds of illnesses. Before long, the water was put on sale. Cheltenham became more popular after King George III visited in 1788. So many visitors came that there was a search for a new well. A number of new spas were created between 1801 and 1825. These included Montpellier Spa, with its magnificent gardens, which was created after 1809, and Sherborne Spa, which was created in 1818.

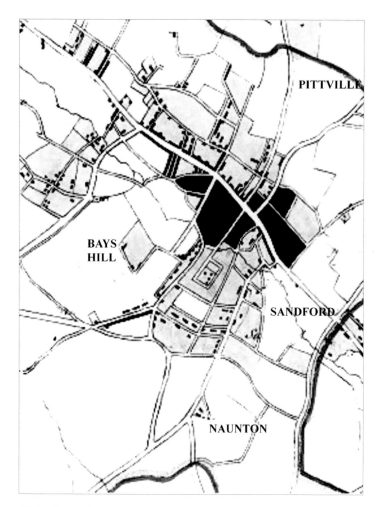

Cheltenham, 1830

In 1801, it had a population of just over 3,000. That may seem tiny by today's standards but by the standards of the time it was a fair-sized market town. However, the population of Cheltenham exploded in the early nineteenth century (for the more pedantic reader, I would like to say that I mean that metaphorically; we did not have some strange explosion removing the entire population of the town). By 1851, the population of Cheltenham had reached 35,000, but population growth eased in the second half of the nineteenth century. Today, Cheltenham is a bustling tourist town with a population of over fifty million; alright, I think I may be prone to exaggeration on that front, but it certainly has increased a large amount over the last few decades.

So, enough of this history lesson! Let us go and find some ghosties.

CHAPTER 1

GHOST WALK 1

This walk is very interesting, as it takes us along a length of the High Street and then continues through a line of buildings — almost as though someone placed a thick ruler on the map and drew a line along it. For those of you that believe in ley-lines, there may be something of interest here.

The Town Hall

If you are lucky, you will be able to get into and walk around the building, which is a fantastic structure. Cheltenham Town Hall was built in 1902-03 as a venue needed for the many balls and concerts, which were the basis for Cheltenham's society enternainment at the turn of the twentieth century; up until that point the role had been fulfilled by the old Assembly Rooms in the High Street. When they were demolished to make way for a bank, the council decided to build a new, much larger hall on a new site.

The site where the town hall stands was a former bowling green and also part of Imperial Square, which back then contained beautiful gardens and a large glass and steel Winter Garden building, which has also now been demolished.

On 1 October 1902, the foundation stone of the building was laid (it can still be seen today on its exterior) by the mayor, George Norman. As was the custom at the time, a bottle containing contemporary coins and copies of local newspapers were placed behind the stone; hopefully, they are still there to this day.

In 1916, two plaster-cast statues of King Edward VII and King George V, both in coronation robes, were placed in alcoves on either side of the main stage. Now, these are probably not the figures that have been seen wandering around when no one should be in the building.

If you walk into the town hall and turn left, you will see a drinks fountain containing the world-famous spa waters of Cheltenham; if you are really brave then try drinking some. Then turn right and you will see a long corridor, and it is this corridor where a shadowy figure has been seen going into some of the rooms off to the side. A few previous members of staff have told me that, at various times, they have seen or heard people walking down this corridor — knowing that there was nobody but themselves in the building.

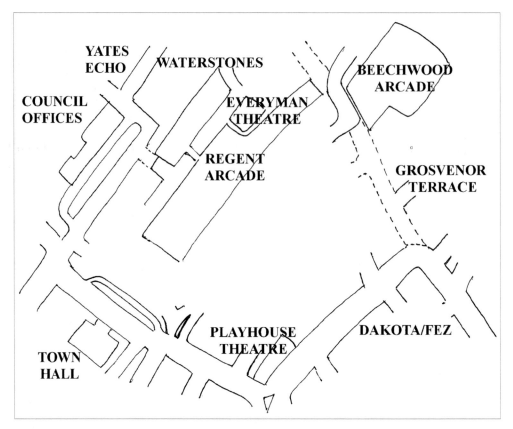

Ghost Walk 1, part 1

The other interesting spook to be found in the building is on the other side of the hall. Go back to the main entrance, this time turn right and go up the stairs (this is not always possible, as the building is not necessarily open to the public all the time). I have heard stories of figures on the right-hand balcony, stories that I can verify myself, as I was once stood at the stage end of this balcony and turned around to see a shadowy figure about ten feet away from me. This then quickly disappeared — leaving me confused and rather scared.

One of my favourite stories about the town hall is not so much supernatural as humorous. Back in 1949, a hypnotist by the name of Peter Casson was giving a demonstration of his skills. He managed to acquire a volunteer from the audience and started pushing pins through the back of her hand. She felt no pain. However, a member of the audience did, as he fainted, fell forwards and broke his nose on the back of the seat in front of him.

Now, standing back outside the town hall, we are only a few hundred yards from our next ghostie. Turn right and walk to the traffic lights. Cross here and turn right again. Now walk all the way to the end of this road and you will be stood outside the Playhouse Theatre.

The Playhouse Theatre

It seems that there have been theatre facilities in some form or other in Cheltenham for quite some time, but for sixty years or so, the people of Cheltenham have enjoyed the fact that they have their own theatre. A theatre in which talented amateurs all work together to present fantastic works of art, to amazingly high standards, to the theatre-going public. Alright, I know I am slightly biased because I have performed there several times myself.

It was while performing there a few months before this book was published that I last experienced anything paranormal. If you go into the main auditorium then you will see two low balconies. I walked under one of these and heard someone walk directly over the top of me; there was no mistaking the sound of footsteps directly above my head. I was looking for the theatre manager and assumed this must be him, as no one else was in the building. I called out to him and started chatting about the production that was on, but after about twenty seconds, I realised there was no one there and no possible way that he could have walked away without passing me. If you are lucky, then you may even get to go on one of the ghost hunts that the theatre puts on every so often.

So, a few words of history here. The mineral springs in Cheltenham, which you will hopefully have been partaking of in the town hall, were discovered in 1716. Back then Cheltenham was merely an ordinary country village, housing not much more than an eleventh-century country church, blacksmith's shop, farmyard, parsonage, village inn (The Plough) and a few thatched cottages along a broad street.

On discovering the mineral springs, the town underwent an amazing and rapid transformation from village into spa. In 1788, His Majesty King George III paid the town a visit to take the waters, and in doing so he gave Cheltenham a significant level of popularity and fame.

Henry Thompson's Montpellier Baths, which is now the Cheltenham Playhouse theatre, opened in 1806 and very soon became a very popular venue to enjoy the therapeutic waters. It contained fourteen warm baths of marble and Dutch tiles; one large cold bath, 20 feet by 10 feet, which was big enough for swimming; and several smaller ones.

On the therapeutic front, Dr Jameson, writing in 1809, claimed Cheltenham waters were good for 'dyspepsia, eruption, pimples, inflammations, exudations, scrofulous affections, ulcers of the legs, opthalmies, rheumatism and gout, asthma and cough, female disease, piles, gravelly disorders and worms'.

Just before the end of the Second World War in 1945, Cheltenham Council realised that there was a lack of theatrical facilities and converted the baths into a theatre. Under the auditorium there is still the original pool, now used as a store room for all the props and costumes.

This amazing theatre was one of my first experiences of haunted buildings. For those of you who do not know me, I am an actor, performer and writer, and back in the '80s, I rented the theatre to put on my first musical, *Frankenstein, No Mrs Andrews, it's not the Movie* — a strange title I know, and an even stranger show. During my time in the theatre, we spent many long days and nights building sets and getting the show ready for performance. It was during this time that I started to get an uneasy feeling about the stage-right area of the theatre.

A friend of mine was the lighting and set designer for many shows there and told me of a figure that he had seen several times on one of the balconies. He also told me about a time that he and a friend were working so late they decided to sleep in one of the dressing rooms. They were both lying there, not in any way drifting off at all, when they heard someone walk down the corridor towards the fire exit and rattle the chains holding the doors closed. It's nice to see that theatre ghosts are so theatrical that they rattle chains!

I always had a very uneasy feeling about certain areas of the theatre, and it was these memories, and my friends' stories, that led me to try and get a full paranormal investigation into the theatre. So, we jump forwards almost twenty years to today and PARASOC's investigation into the Playhouse theatre.

I will not print the full report given by the PARASOC group, as it is very technical and goes into immense detail about what equipment is used, and it would take up the rest of the book. Instead, I shall give you the highlights of what happened.

The very first investigation we did into this building provided a few intriguing results. Unfortunately, however, it provided nothing concrete on tape or film.

As per usual, we split into groups on arrival and walked around the building doing an experiment on sensory mapping (plotting out where we all thought the freaky, weird places were — a highly technical term there but I am sure you can grasp the idea). The groups all marked on maps where they thought spooky stuff had happened

Ghost hunt at the Playhouse

in the past. Then we regrouped in order to be given various areas to investigate throughout the evening.

The evening then became more exciting. The groups spread out around the building to try and record anything unusual happening, which it did in abundance. One of the areas that the sensory mapping had thrown up as potentially interesting was a small area in the corner to the left of the stage. This area is where ladders are kept tied to a wall. About an hour into the investigation, these ladders started to shake. None of them were loose, but continually, throughout the evening, they would start rattling away in the corner until someone went to investigate. Now, these ladders are very large and heavy — we are not talking about an aluminium three-foot step ladder, these ladders are big enough to reach the lights above the stage, which is at least twelve feet, and need two people to move them. We also accounted for everyone who was in the building and their whereabouts, so we knew full well that none of our ghost hunters could, for some strange reason, be shaking the ladders.

One of our ghost hunters did a head count to see how many of us were in the auditorium at one point, and she counted six people. It was not until later that she realised there were only five people in the auditorium. It was then pointed out that this was a regular occurrence, with extra people being seen in the theatre who are not really there.

This was not the only extra person sighted in the theatre, as a figure was seen on the balcony (on the left-hand side if you are stood looking out from the stage). When our intrepid ghost buster realised there should not have been anyone there they turned around to see that the balcony was empty yet again. There was no way that anyone could have passed them to walk from the balcony area. This area also proved to be very interesting the second time we investigated. Paul and I were sat in the theatre waiting for anything to happen when we both heard strange noises emanating from the balcony. I was looking at a bank of monitors and saw Paul turn to look at the area at exactly the same time as I heard something there. This happened a few times, and yet the night-vision cameras we had on the balcony showed that there was nothihng up there. When Paul turned his camera towards the balcony, the light on top of is camera came on full blast and a bright beam of light pulsed out from the camera, which shocked him slightly as he was not touching it, just the camera stand that it was on. He turned the light off and we watched the eight-hour battery drain to nothing in a matter of seconds. About half an hour later he managed to turn the camera back on, with a large amount of battery power indicating on the screen.

Another intriguing story that is often told of the Playhouse concerns floating blue lights in the main auditorium. Two investigators from PARASOC saw these lights, which were floating halfway back through the auditorium. There is a slight problem in investigating this phenomenon, as the floor level has been raised. This means that, in theory, the strange lights should be beneath floor level. However, when we have investigated underneath the floor since, we have not seen any lights.

This was not the end of our first investigation. Another area of interest that we investigated was the back stairs. It later transpired that these stairs are indeed of particular interest; many times people have heard mysterious footsteps on the back stairs and doors opening when there is nobody else in the building. Our second investigation involved us taking along a bunch of new ghost hunters that had no idea

Ben being attacked by orbs at the Playhouse
Investigation

about the stories involving the staircase. When they were sat on the first floor, quietly waiting for anything to happen, they heard, a couple of times, people walking up the stairs and opening doors. They assumed it was one of us and ignored it. We proved to them that none of us were in the area of the stairs, as we had a video camera recording in there all the time. We also had an audio recorder but, oddly, it picked up no noise at all.

These are not all the stories associated with this building — just the ones that we managed in some small way to experience through our investigations. Many other people talk of the figure on the balcony and the noises on the back stairs.

To finish off with, one interesting story I know of involves a phantom member of the cast during a show. One member of the audience watched a show and afterwards walked up to the director and said that he liked the show but could not understand the relevance of the young girl who was stood on the stage to the right. The director looked justifiably bemused and replied that there was no child on the stage.

This is not the only ghost castmember who has been seen, as once there was a band on the stage for a production when a woman walked on and said something to the drummer. When questioned afterwards as to what it was that the woman said, everyone looked confused and said, 'What woman?'

As you stand with your back to the door of the Playhouse, turn left and head towards the High Street area of town. You will notice a gateway to a park on your right-hand side and then after this you will see a pub and a nightclub. It is the nightclub that we are interested in next. Cross carefully at the lights and then head towards Dakota (at the time of writing this book the club was called Dakota, but clubs change their name so often, it may well be something else).

The Fez Club (Dakota)

We investigated this nightclub back when it was called The Fez Club and had some rather interesting and mixed results. We were told of strange happenings that would go on in the darker upstairs back bar, but then it is a nightclub and strange things do go on in dark nightclubs. We arrived with a team of intrepid ghost busters, armed with thousands of pounds worth of ghost-hunting equipment, which up until that point had registered nothing that warranted the bank loans and overdrafts needed to buy them.

We (PARASOC) started the evening by doing a sensory mapping experiment, and whilst walking around, I was being filmed by a cameraman. Now, we got very excited when we heard a strange tinkling noise and banging of metal from the bottom of a staircase that we were filming on. However, our excitement soon turned to disappointment when we reached the bottom of the stairs and found that it was highly likely that one of us had accidentally knocked some broken glass down the stairs, where it would have rebounded off a lot of metal bars on its way down.

This club is a large building operating on two floors, and there have been buildings here for quite a while. Historically speaking, we had a lot to cover and, floor-space-wise, a lot to monitor. We set up many cameras all over the place, and thermometers, sound recorders and data-logging equipment. All these, for several hours, showed us an amazing amount of... nothing. We decided to concentrate our efforts instead. We were unaware of the stories attached to the place, but through the sensory mapping experiment, we had decided to concentrate our efforts in one area, the upstairs back bar. We had three night-vision cameras being operated and voice recorders running in various areas. One of the cameras seemed to pick up a lot of orbs in night vision (I will explain orbs in detail later on).

Despite the excitement of small white floating objects on the screen, we felt there was not much happening. Paul (a veteran PARASOC investigator) was getting slightly annoyed by the occasional talking and laughing that was going on behind him. Now, if he had turned around, he may have got slightly more excited as he would have realised there was no one behind him — all of us were in front of him. Unfortunately, even though Paul was operating a video camera, the talking and mumbling was too faint to be captured by the camera microphone and we did not have any audio recorders in that part of the room.

The group were very nearly in need of new trousers when an almighty noise startled them all. This turned out to be an ice machine that went off every hour or so. Many a hardened ghost hunter has been sent screaming from a room, only to return and find out the air conditioner had just kicked in or the pipes make a strange rattling noise. On a side note, one of the most scary places we have ever investigated was a place in Abergavenny on top of Mount Blorange in a pub called the Lamb and Fox. Bruce (all the names I am going to mention in this story belong to PARASOC investigators, all of whom I have known for years and have no reason to make anything up or lie) was particularly on edge this evening, and he and Jenny went into a haunted part of the pub, which, unfortunately for them, was the toilets. They became very scared when something growled at them and they scrambled trying to open the door for ages; we have some very humorous footage of two people trying to open a door, swearing profusely and getting more and more scared. When Justin and myself went into the toilets, we soon discovered the same growl — which was an automatic air freshener that went off every twenty minutes or so.

With three night-vision cameras and many voice recorders around, we were confident, but nothing really happened until about 2 a.m. At this point, we started shouting out to the ghosts to do something, as we were getting bored. Five minutes after this, a plastic pint glass lifted from the bar, got scrunched up and then fell onto the floor behind the bar. There were a couple of people who saw it, all of us heard it and all of us could account for where we were. Nobody was behind the bar where it had happened. So I asked the question 'who managed to film it?' Unfortunately, no one did, as they were all looking in different directions. So, we had the audio recording of a flying cup, followed by lots of expletives, but no actual video evidence.

This tied in with some of the stories we were later told; apparently, this area was where unexplained occurences had been previously reported. Also, the toilets next to the bar are where mysterious figures have been seen in the past.

With your back to the nightclub, turn right and head towards the High Street, follow the road around the corner until you get to the traffic lights. Cross the road here and turn right, heading out of town until you reach the pub on the right that used to be called O'Hagan's but at the time of writing is the Swan.

O'Hagan's (The Swan)

When I was a student desperately struggling for cash, I ended up having to work behind a bar, as most students do. When I worked behind this bar it was called O'Hagan's. Now, in my time working there, we had a problem with taps turning themselves on and off, but not a huge amount of spookiness otherwise. Before I worked there, however, the situation was something different altogether.

A friend of mine used to work and live there, and she told me she was once cleaning the bar after the place was closed when she felt as though someone was watching her. She turned around to see a man standing behind her. I asked her to describe what the apparition looked like, but she said that she did not stick around long enough to find out! She also told me of the many times that, when in one of the flats upstairs, she had heard someone walk up the stairs. Whenever she had gotten up to investigate, however, there was never anybody there.

Another friend of mine who used to work there told me that often, when lying in bed, she had heard someone walk into the flat. Slightly panicked, she would get up to investigate — only to find that the flat was empty.

At one point, a paranormal investigation group (not PARASOC) were called in to have a go at contacting spirits at O'Hagan's. This was done due to the fact that a figure had been seen in the 'snug' area of the bar (later seen on camera but — surprise surprise — it was not recording). If the snug area is taken then it is worth walking to the back of the pub and sitting quietly listening for footsteps from upstairs. I have been in the pub knowing that upstairs was empty and yet have still heard footsteps. I mentioned this to a few regulars and they confirmed that I was not the first to comment on this.

Head back in the direction you came from towards town, and within a few hundred yards, you will come across another haunted pub, this one, at the time of writing, is called the Restoration or Varsity at the Restoration.

The Restoration

I have been told by someone who used to frequent this pub many years ago of the figure of a young girl who floats along the corridor upstairs and also of an upstairs room where items mysteriously disappear for long periods of time. The girl may be responsible for moving the items, and she may also be the noisy spirit that makes the occasional knocking or banging noise.

With your back to the Restoration turn right and walk towards the pedestrian area of the upper High Street. As you continue to walk through town, you will see a small alleyway leading off through an arch to the right, this heads up to a large car park, gym and supermarket. Before you reach the delights of the supermarket, you will notice a few small shops on the right, hopefully there will be a very nice man there who still runs his butcher's shop, directly above which was my old flat. This building, many years ago, used to be the original Theatre Royal.

Grosvenor Terrace (The Old Theatre Royal)

Now, on this spot many years ago stood the Theatre Royal, and you will see a plaque on the wall denoting this fact. This can be found next to the doors that lead upstairs to the flats, one of which is haunted by a poltergeist called George. Now, how do I know it's haunted, and, more importantly, how do I know the poltergeist is called George? Well, the answer is that I once lived there, and I named him.

My favourite story involving George is all about sweets at Christmas. As all ghost stories should be, it is set on Christmas Eve. I have always been a huge fan of Christmas, and even as an adult, my friends and family would give each other Christmas stockings that obviously came from the big man himself, Santa Claus. In the stockings were little presents and sweets. I was living with a girlfriend at the time, and I had bought some silly tubes of sweets with some flashing reindeers on the top. By flashing I mean they had red lights in the noses of the reindeers and not that they were wearing large raincoats and exposing themselves to you on command.

Well, these tubes of small, multi-coloured sweets were completely sealed, and on Christmas Eve I placed them into the stocking; on Christmas morning they were found, along with many items, but not actually consumed or even opened, so by Christmas night they were still sealed and not touched. On Boxing Day morning, we awoke to find the sweets had all gone, yet the tubes were still sealed. We found this rather bizarre, yet for some reason, we thought no more of it. A few months later, it was all brought bouncing back to us, quite literally.

A friend of mine was staying at my house for a few days, and the pair of us were online trying to buy some tickets for something when we heard a tapping noise. This then stopped, only to start again a few minutes later. It continued to stop and start a couple of times, and then, the next time it started, we turned around to see a small sweet bouncing along the floor towards us. This happened again five minutes later; I picked up the sweet to notice that it was the same type of sweet that had disappeared from the sealed tube. We never saw where the sweets were coming from, as they only appeared when neither of us were looking, and had our backs to the room, I hasten to add that we were the only people in the room and that there was no way there could have been anyone hiding and throwing sweets at us without our knowledge.

It was in this house that I started to dabble in orb photography. For many years, people have been claiming that orbs on digital cameras are the first manifestation of spirits. Personally, I think that this is not the case but that they are actually the first manifestation of dust and insects. Now, even though I have discredited orbs in the past, we did take some very interesting photographs here. We would pose and hold out a hand saying, 'Alright then George, appear next to my hand' and, low and behold, an orb would be right at the end of the hand. If you are interested in orb photography, then that is the only way you can prove any intelligence behind them.

Now back onto the pedestrians part of the High Street and turn right, you will very soon reach the Beechwood Arcade, walk into the arcade and head towards the back of it, near the escalators.

Beechwood Arcade (MVC, Debenhams)

I have a love of music, so a job I thoroughly enjoyed was working in a record store. This store, MVC, was at the back of the Beechwood Arcade. In the mornings, we would be downstairs getting everything ready. Upstairs would have a large, metal fence-type door that could only be raised using a key or — a very time-consuming method — by winding a handle from the inside.

As I was sat downstairs with one of the supervisors one day, we looked at the screen of the CCTV to see someone on the shop floor. We assumed that somehow we had left the gate open and went running upstairs to see... absolutely no one. Not only was there nobody there, the gate was still in the locked position, and there was nowhere for anyone to have gone without setting off the fire-exit alarms. Unfortunately, the CCTV was not actually recording at the time, so we kept the story to ourselves for fear of being branded as weird — or at least weirder than most people thought we were anyway.

I have also heard of another spectre not too far away from this one. I was not told too much about it except for the fact that it is a shadowy figure that walks around the storage areas of Debenhams, occasionally moving stock around. I am sure that he is not on the payroll and does not officially work there, as working after death definitely classes as overtime.

Now from one arcade to another, turn right out of the Beechwood Arcade and very soon you will reach the Regent Arcade, on the other side of the road. Now stand with your back to the Regent Arcade and to your left, on the other side of the High Street, you will see a small entrance to a nightclub, which was called Time for quite a long time. We will have a quick look at this place before we go into Regent Arcade.

Time

(These stories relate to when the nightclub was called TIME)
Now, these stories are a few years old, as I obtained them from previous staff who worked at Time about ten years ago. They tell stories of a ghost of a child that wandered around the club. I often wonder how many people see ghosts in a place where they expect to see something like that and therefore assume the ghost is a real person. Let us take, for, a ghost of a young man walking down the High Street in jeans and a T-shirt a example nd then turning down an alleyway. Now, unless it is the middle of winter and snowing, this would seem perfectly normal. A child in a nightclub is obviously not an expected sight. The child, to my knowledge, has never been seen when the place is full, only when locking up or before the place is opened. The child seems to be quite mischievous and moves things around, and one previous waitress from years ago tells how the knives and forks would rearrange themselves when you were not looking. *Now let's head into Regent Arcade.*

Regent Arcade (Toy Shop, Athena, First Floor Shop)

High Street Entrance
In my time, I have worked in several shops in Cheltenham, a few of which were in the Regent Arcade. Whilst I was there, I heard of three interesting stories relating to paranormal activity. One of these took place in the toy shop that used to be found up the escalator as you walk in on the left from the High Street.

This area of the arcade used to be a coach house going back hundreds of years, so if anywhere should be haunted, it is a distinct possibility this place will be.

I was told of a ghost that inhabited the toy store's main storage room, rocking horses that were seen to move of their own accord and things that would move about, only to be later found elsewhere. I was also told of a previous member of staff who went into the storeroom and then came suddenly storming out of the room. Not talking to anyone, she hurriedly left the store, not even returning to get her coat. She apparently could not be coaxed back to work and quit saying she would never go there again. She refused to ever say what it was that she saw.

Ground Floor Shop
In the shop that was Athena, about halfway down the arcade on the left-hand side, one of the workers told us that on some steps a figure had been seen. She did not follow to

Regent Arcade

The Plough Hotel

see who it was, as she was shaking too much. Soon after, however, it happened again, and this time, a braver member of staff followed — to find no one there.

First Floor Shop

The third story is about one of the upstairs shops between the double escalator and the large department store at the rear of the arcade (at the time of writing this was TK Maxx). One of the security guards was rather shaken by the female apparition that seemed to be working behind the till of the locked shop. He was more shocked as they seemed to be wearing something that looked like an old-fashioned bathing cap. The image soon disappeared, as did all rational thought, and to this day I am sure he can't give a decent explanation for what he saw.

The Fire Exit — Ground floor

If you have walked in through the High Street entrance this is behind some of the shops at the back near the Regent Street entrance; sorry, this is not one you will get a chance to look for. Years ago a man died by falling from the car park and landing outside the fire exit area, after which the sound of someone outside the doors was often heard. However, if you opened the doors, the noise stopped, and nobody was ever actually there.

As you walk out of the Regent Street entrance to the arcade, turn right and walk back towards the High Street. Before you reach the pedestrian area, you will see the Everyman Theatre on your right-hand side.

The Everyman Theatre

The Everyman Theatre was originally opened as The New Theatre and Opera House on 1 October 1891. It has the distinction of being the oldest, still-working Frank Matcham-designed theatre in the country, and, as one actor put it, 'When you stand on the Everyman stage and look out, it's like you are acting inside a pink iced wedding cake.'

The theatre had a truly amazing opening, with the most famous actress of that, or any other, era, Lily Langtry. She recited an introductory prologue praising the brand-new building and then went on to star in Tom Taylor's play *Lady Clancarty*, as produced by her own theatre company.

In the beginning, the theatre staged a variety of entertainment, including classical plays, serious drama and the world-famous The D'Oyly Carte Opera Company. Famous actors, such as Ellen Terry, H. B. Irving and even Charlie Chaplin, appeared at the theatre.

The Second World War brought great theatrical opportunities and even greater stars to Cheltenham when all the theatres in London closed during the Blitz. Cheltenham, largely escaping the bombing, offered some of the only opportunities for actors to continue to perform. Laurence Olivier visited the town, as did Donald Wolfit and John Gielgud. Later audiences were lucky enough to watch young stars perform in some of their first public appearances. Steven Berkoff played at the Everyman in his early career, and Harold Pinter performed under his acting name. Other famous actors, such as Windsor Davies and Penelope Keith, have also performed there. Since then, it has become a touring theatre, once more attracting huge film and television names.

So we have heard about the amazing talent that has graced the boards of this theatre, but what about the not-so-alive regular guest? I have often performed at this theatre, and I was told once that no other actor since the refurbishments a quarter of a decade ago has performed there more than I have. In total, I was in about thirty-five different shows here, so you would think that I may have experienced a few ghosties myself. Unfortunately, however, the only one that I ever sensed was on the top corridor. A lot of the staff who work here often say they do not like this corridor, but then it is very high up and the wind rattles across it causing eerie noises. The strange thing about this part of the building is that it is actually quite new. It is at the rear of the building, where all the scenery flies up into the roof of the theatre.

One fantastical story about this part of the building is from when it was being renovated and the stage was covered in scaffolding all the way to the roof. Roger, a well-known member of staff at the theatre, tells how one night they could see people running around the scaffolding and making noises. They called the police, who turned up with a police dog. They called up to the figures that could be seen up

The Everyman Theatre

there, and when they had no response, they headed up the scaffolding with the dog in tow. The dog, however, soon turned around and scampered out of the building, and no actual people could be found. You may think they somehow escaped, but I can honestly say that there is no possible way of getting out of the building. If they had managed to get out of the roof, then they would have been so high up that there would be nowhere to go — except very fast towards the pavement below. (This was before they had built Regent Arcade, and it was all just an empty car park at the back of the theatre.)

A colleague of mine tells a tale of how he was taking photographs for a production, and at the dress rehearsal he decided to get higher up and take some shots. He walked up the side fire-exit stairs to get to the top level and instead walked out onto the upper circle. There he saw a figure looking down at the stage. He quickly turned around, thinking 'well, I don't want to disturb him', and carried on up to the next floor. It was then that he started to have strange thoughts, thinking that he could not really remember what the figure looked like. Within ten seconds he was on the next floor and looked down to see that the man had gone. It later transpired that the doors were locked and the figure would have had to go past me to get out.

It may also be this ghost that has been spotted a few times by people walking up to the top of the building to their seats. They see a man, sometimes with a cap on, in front of them, but when they look again, there is no one there. This has been spotted by one of my ghost-hunting colleagues as well as by cast members of shows that I have been in.

I will get back to some reports from years gone by at the theatre, but first I would like to tell you of PARASOC's report on the building. I will not relate the entire report, as it is about 50,000 words long, but will tell you all the interesting parts.

PARASOC did an investigation at the theatre along with John Rockley of BBC radio Gloucestershire. As with most ghost hunts in commercial buildings, it was a lot to do with publicity. The fantastic supernatural play *The Woman in Black* was also touring there (if you have not seen it yet, then you really must). It all started out as most ghost hunts do: rather uneventful. We had our fair share of orbs appear on cameras but, as I have said, we do not hold much store by them. The first hour of the investigation was spent setting up experiments and doing baseline readings. One experiment we set up was to place some coins on some card and then drop talcum powder over them. This meant that if the coins were moved by a spirit we would know about it, and, more importantly, if the coins were moved by real person then we would see the fingerprints. We also set up some hidden cameras in lockable rooms, which was done so that we knew nobody could affect them. We had a large group of people with us and all were raring to go and ready to see what the theatre would throw at us, which, in my previous experience of ghost hunting, was likely to be very little.

Because there were so many of us and the building was so big, we split into many groups. Unfortunately for me, as I knew the layout of the building very well, my job was to take groups around the theatre and leave them in their allotted places for half an hour. This meant that, by the time I got to my position with my group, I had already done two laps of the building. Now, by the last time we did this, everyone knew where they were heading, so, instead of showing people where to go, my group went first and set off down the steps to the area underneath the stage. I was telling my group all about a show I was in where a friend of mine fell through the stage. He was a very big man, well over six feet tall, and had a waist measurement that equalled about two of me.

As I pointed to the area where the stage gave way, we heard a loud thumping noise, which was coming directly from where I was pointing. The group of four intrepid ghost hunters came running up the stairs and onto the stage, hoping to see what it was. We saw nothing, and then moments later a group came into the theatre as they were going to be investigating the stage area. We asked them if they had made the noise or if any other group had walked across the stage, and they said that, apart from us, everyone else was in the café area.

We got very excited, as we realised that we had left a video camera running in the auditorium. Surely, that would show us what made the noise. We eagerly played the tape back, putting the volume up high. On the recording you can clearly hear me telling everyone the story of my friend crashing through the stage, and then, a few seconds later, you can hear all of us asking each other if we had heard the thumping noise. The amazing thing is that, no matter how much you turn up the volume, you cannot hear the thump, which means all four of us experienced the same auditory hallucination at the same time.

Next, myself, a few other ghost busters and John Rockley decided to head into the cellar, which I was told was a very spooky place. It was certainly cramped and not particularly pleasant. Yet, within about a minute of being down there, we all got a massive fit of the giggles that did not stop until we were dragged out of the place. Not exactly supernatural, more like a nervous reaction, but I have never laughed so much in my life.

My group then headed into the workshop area. As we walked in, we spoke that classic line 'Is there anybody there?' There was an immediate response: a loud, metallic bang. We asked the same question again and got another loud bang in response. Then a large ball of light went between myself and Justin, who was walking about ten feet in front of me. We could not get any more responses from our questions, and we had a good look around to check that there was nobody hiding in there playing tricks on us.

As we walked out of the workshop, we crossed the stage to hear a siren go off. We all looked up and saw a member of the theatre staff waving at us and telling us to come upstairs to the upper circle. She had set off our motion detector alarms, as she did not have a radio and thought it was the best way to get our attention. It transpires that she had walked into that area and seen several orangey balls of light floating near the coins that we had put in there. When we looked at the coins, they had all moved, not a massive amount, only about a centimetre at most, but enough to think that natural vibrations would not have cause it. The full report goes into a few other photographic anomalies but nothing to really be able to substantially report as paranormal.

We would love to get back into this building and have another go, but the trouble with all the interesting theatres is that they have shows on all the time, so its very difficult to get into them. Before we leave the subject of haunted theatres, I will add one more story just to humiliate a friend of mine. We were to give a talk on how to hunt ghosts in a theatre, on their main stage, and then run a ghost hunting night.

Bruce was driving us there, and the group who booked us asked him if he wanted the postcode to put into his Sat Nav, to which he replied, 'Don't worry about it, I will look it up.'

Now, from Cheltenham to Nottingham theatre is not a short journey, so we set off nice and early, and early enough that, if the traffic was with us, we would get there with a few hours to spare to be able to get around the building and do a spot of ghost hunting without anyone else present. We pulled up on a very busy road, not sure of how to get in, and decided to phone the people who had booked us. We told them we were standing outside under a huge poster for *Cats*. They sounded confused and said, 'So long as you are standing outside the Northampton Derngate theatre, we will be able to find you.' At this point, Bruce went bright red and said, 'We will call you back.' We then turned the car around and headed south again to Northampton. Thankfully, we had given ourselves those extra hours, as we turned up just fifteen minutes before going on stage.

Another story told by Roger is of an old painting that used to hang backstage, and every time the painting was taken down, a disaster would happen, the biggest of which was when the building was being closed down for renovation. The painting was removed, and as they locked the building, the back wall of the theatre just collapsed, leaving a large gaping hole.

During a few performances, the figure of a woman walking stage right (that's the left-hand side for the audience and right-hand side for the actors) has been seen backstage. She walks along and then hangs something on a coat stand. Other times she has been seen just walking and then disappearing. The audience never seem to see her, as she is just offstage, but various cast members have seen her, even during performances.

Theatres always seem to give us a lot of stories, but the one I would love to hear is the ghostly orchestra that plays in here. Several staff have been locking up the building when they have heard music emanating from the auditorium, but as soon as they open the doors to find out what is going on, the music stops. So, if you are ever sat in the café during the daytime thinking there is a fantastic show or concert being performed, it may be the Everyman Theatre's ghost orchestra.

Opposite the Everyman Theatre is the rear entrance to Cavendish House, which was once a large, and some thought posh, department store, but now it is a glorified shopping arcade, with miniature versions of High Street stores in it.

Cavendish House

Cavendish House is actually the town's oldest department store. The store was opened in 1823 as one of the provincial branches of Cavendish House (these were originally called Clark and Debenham), a London-based drapery business run by Thomas Clark and William Debenham.

The premises were refurbished a number of times in the 1800s, whilst remaining largely in the same location. The most substantial refurbishment was in 1931, with the creation of its distinctive Art Deco pre-Brutalist 287-foot frontage on the Promenade. A lot of Cheltonians consider it a rather ugly blemish on the town's Regency face.

Cavendish House

The entrances on Regent Street retain the older Victorian and Art Nouveau stylings. The inside of building remains a maze of staircases and rooms, a throwback to all the layouts of the various expansions.

There is an old story about the lift here, so get into the lift before you read the next bit; it may make it slightly scarier.

A nice short story for you, as hopefully you are in the lift on your own. Turn around and see if you have been joined by an old woman; we have been told she likes to spend her afterlife shopping but does not want to use the stairs.

Another story concerns a storeroom area, in the front basement, where staff have seen a figure walking around, yet when you get close to it, it disappears.

Walk out of the exit for Cavendish on the other side of the building, leading onto the Promenade, and you will be facing Waterstones, the book store. This was not always Waterstone's and has had various other uses throughout its time.

The sculpture by Sophie Ryder, outside Waterstone's

Waterstone's Book Shop

I do hope you are reading this book whilst stood in this beautiful building, which is an intriguing shape and has a central tower of a staircase circling up the middle of it (do walk up and down this staircase and see if you can sense anything). I have heard tales dating back for quite a while of a figure seen on here. This ties in with previous users of this building that told of a mysterious figure walking around.

With your back to Waterstone's, turn left and head towards the road. At the road turn right and you will see a large entrance to the Yates's's building, which was once the entrance to the Gloucestershire Echo *offices.*

The old *Echo* building; now Yates's

Echo/Yates's

Stories about this building have been hard to come by, but when the Yates's building used to be part of the *Echo* building, I was given tales of strange noises and footsteps — when you looked up there was nobody there. It also seems as though Yates's has the same restless phantom. Tales have been reported to me from previous members of staff about mysterious footsteps going up the stairs, so perhaps, even though the building's occupants moved next door, the ghosts did not.

Standing on the steps of Yates's, turn right and walk around the corner. You will see the Echo *buildings along the entire length of this road right up to the traffic lights, but over the road you will see a converted church, now a bar called Revolution.*

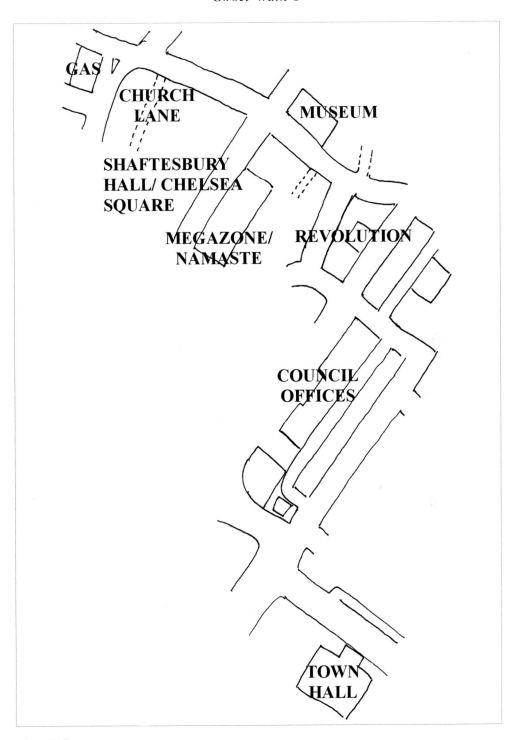

GAS

CHURCH
LANE

MUSEUM

SHAFTESBURY
HALL/ CHELSEA
SQUARE

MEGAZONE/
NAMASTE

REVOLUTION

COUNCIL
OFFICES

TOWN
HALL

Ghost Walk 1, part 2

Revolution, the bar

Revolution

There have been many reports of glasses that would move on their own and also of people having an uneasy feeling, as though being watched, when in the upstairs bar at this venue.

One Hallowe'en, we tried to do a daytime broadcast from inside this building. Everything would be working perfectly but as soon as we tried to go over to the studio it would all stop working again. We would establish a line again, and then the studio would hand over to us to hear absolutely nothing. So, giving up on trying to broadcast live from inside, we went outside. Everything was working fine but, again, as soon as the studio tried to hand over to us, it all went wrong again. We changed location to another venue and it happened again, and a third time as well. It was as if something didn't want BBC Radio Gloucestershire listeners to get frightened that day.

Walk out of Revolution and turn left. Walk around the corner and head towards the large Gothic-looking church building; just before it you will notice a small drive, you cannot walk down there as it is private property, but I will tell you a small tale about it.

The Countryside Comission

Now, this is a difficult one as you can't actually see this building, but there was once an office belonging to the countryside commission and, at one point in its history, it also belonged to a poltergeist.

We have various reports of items being moved and lights going on and off. As I said, I cannot tell you too much, as you can't get into this building. The reason I know of some of the stories is because I used to work in a building whose back wall backed onto this property, and I walked around one day to see what was behind our haunted building (which I will tell you all about in the next section). Someone came up to us to question what we were doing there, so we explained about our ghost. In turn, they started to tell us all about mysterious figures seen and objects moving seemingly on their own in their building. Unfortunately, we did not get to investigate this building but the building behind it, however, we did.

Before we get to that building, let's take a look at the museum. Over the road you can see the museum and art gallery. You can easily add an hour or two to your walk by heading into this fantastic building.

The Museum

Cheltenham Art Gallery and Museum covers a huge scope of subjects, including history, archaeology, paintings, and arts and crafts. There is also a section on Edward Wilson, Cheltenham's Antarctic explorer who died alongside Scott. Many of the paintings featured in the gallery are donated by various people of Cheltenham.

The art gallery was opened in 1899 when the 3rd Baron de Ferrieres, a former mayor and M.P. for Cheltenham, gave forty-three paintings to the town. In 1905, the museum opened when the Schools of Art and Science vacated the rooms next to the gallery.

In 1989, the Princess Royal opened an extension to the art gallery and museum, which is where the present entrance is located. Our hopes were high as we asked previous staff if there had been any paranormal occurences in the building. We thought that the large ornate building, which has a long history, would give us something to get our teeth into. However, the art gallery and museum proved to us that you should never assume anything about a building; just because a place looks like it should have a ghost doesn't mean it necessarily does. There appears to have been just one incident asscoiated with this particular building. A member of staff told us that they were locking up late one night with another member of staff when they both heard someone walking up the large staircase in the middle of the building. They were rather perturbed at this, as there should not have been anyone in the building at the time. They waited just around the corner at the top of the stairs, hoping to jump out and catch whoever was there. The footsteps stopped, and out came the staff members ready to accost the intruders — but there was nobody waiting there. As far as we know, this is the one and only story in the museum, but believe me, it is still well worth a visit. See if you can find the ghost on the stairs, but also, more importantly, give yourself a few hours to walk around this fascinating building.

Carry on walking, with the church building on your left and the library over the road. You will then walk around the corner onto St George's Street. Behind this church building you will find an old warehouse-style building, the ground floor of which has (at the time of writing) two restaurants, Namaste and the Thai Emerald.

Megazone (Now Namaste and the Thai Emerald)

Many years ago, these buildings used to be a laser arena and arcade; if you have ever played at one of these laser arena places, you will know that it is generally described as a large maze in the dark, full of lasers and smoke machines. Now, anyone is going to assume that someone in a dark smoke-filled environment being chased and shot at is going to feel slightly paranoid and scared. However, I have to insist that this is definitely one of the most haunted buildings I have ever been in.

My first strange experience in the building was whilst walking around the maze section, checking everything was working and turning on the lights and smoke machines. It used to take a smoke machine five minutes to warm up, so I sat myself down and waited so that I could operate the machine. I was in no hurry, so I lay on the floor looking up at the ceiling, killing time.

All of a sudden, I felt as though I was lying in a grave and people were staring at me — weird but, there we are, I am a weird person. So, rather scared, I jumped up feeling bizarre and ran for the exit. I managed to get up a whole three steps when it suddenly felt like a brick wall was pushing against me. It didn't hurt but did physically stop me from moving. At the same time, a small girl of about ten or eleven appeared fully formed next to me, on my right. She had black hair and was crying and behind her, about two metres away, were a couple of adult figures, which were too hazy to see properly.

This all happened in the space of only about five seconds, yet it seemed to last a lifetime. I was, as it is known in ghost-hunting circles, scared (the politest word I could think of at this point; there are many more but I am not sure my publisher would allow them!). As soon as I could move again, I ran through the maze, out through a large tunnel and into the foyer area, which is where the amusement arcade section was.

A colleague, who happened to be working behind the counter that day, looked at me and said, 'What's wrong? You look as if you have seen a ghost'. It's not hard to work out what my response was. 'I have, just now.' I fully expected him to be as fascinated as I am now with the subject and come rushing in with video cameras, EMF meters and Dictaphones. I was not let down, for he looked at me with amazement in his eyes and said, 'Yeah right, you prat' — what I now know to be called in ghost-busting circles the standard 'you're an idiot' response.

I was not to be deterred without telling him where and what had just happened. I told him to walk through the maze and just tell me if it felt weird anywhere. He dutifully did this and came out and drew on the map where, if he was to make up a ghost story, he thought it would be set. To my amazement, and his, I showed him the map that I had drawn on whilst he was in the maze; they matched perfectly. I later went on to use this technique to great effect in my investigations, and it is known as sensory mapping.

For those wishing to eat in a haunted restaurant then this area was halfway along the raised area on the left-hand side of the Thai restaurant.

The Thai Emerald

This was the first of any experiences reported in these buildings but not the last. Eventually, one member of staff had to leave as they would not go into certain areas of the building on their own because of paranormal happenings they had experienced.

By the time I left the building, there must have been at least fifty people who had seen, heard, felt, and experienced unexplainable paranormal happenings. My first confirmation that I was not going mad was when myself and a guy called Adrian were installing an old arcade machine. We used to play the games the whole way through to make sure they were working properly — and also because it was a lot of fun. We had been playing for about thirty minutes, and it was about two in the morning, when all of a sudden, a girl's voice said something (neither of us were really sure what). We both turned around and looked directly behind us at exactly the same time.

'There, you heard that,' I said, 'it's not just me being mental then is it?' I was at last thankful that someone else had experienced something.

'To tell you the truth I have heard her a few times but I was too scared to tell anyone in case they thought I was weird,' Adrian replied. I hasten to add that Adrian is not weird but a very nice guy and one that you could trust to tell you the truth. Once we started telling people of this voice, many of the staff and customers started to come forward with their own stories — all of them too scared to have been the first to tell anyone.

I was sitting late one night in the briefing room, which was a small room used to explain the rules of the laser game to people before they went in. Yet again, it was about 2.00 a.m. when I heard the same voice as before and then another female voice reply. The voices were very quiet, so I could not make out exactly what was being said. The only female in the whole building was sitting talking to me, and she then asked me if I had heard what she had just heard. She was rather sacred at this point and called for a taxi home.

Two in the morning turned out to be an interesting time for the ghost population of the Megazone building. They found a great game to play that involved them setting off the fire exit alarms. This normally happened every few days at about 2 in the morning. Thankfully, we normally worked very late, and I would reset the alarms after walking around the maze to check that nobody had actually broken in. On several occasions, all the doors had actually been opened.

We would always have to walk around the maze to check no one had snuck in, and we worked out a way of four people walking across the maze so that nobody could hide. We were doing this one night, when a couple of the staff shouted that they had seen someone running up the ramp. There was a large ramp that lead up to a bridge, and we sent staff up both sides and had staff on the floor — so there was no way anyone could escape unseen. The members of staff all met in the middle of the bridge looking very confused, all wondering where this person had disappeared to. Now, if he was a burglar then he had managed to turn invisible and let himself out without setting the alarms off again. The ramp area where this apparition was seen was where I had also seen the first ghost of the crying girl.

Another apparition that I had first-hand experience of did not feel scary at all; in fact, it felt as though these ghosts were checking to see if I was alright. I was sat down on the floor with my back to the large metal doors in the kit room, where we kept all the laser guns and equipment. I became very aware that there were two people in the room with me — nothing unusual about that, as often people would come in to get their battery changed in their guns — I looked up at them and saw that they had no features and were more like silhouettes, and had no legs from below the knee. One of them seemed to bend down to where I was sitting, and it felt as though they were seeing if I was OK. Then, suddenly, they disappeared just as I tried to say something to them.

A story which we all found fascinating and which led us, yet again, to have to search the building was all about a man in a cupboard. In the kit room there was a small cupboard-like alcove that had a sliding door. We used to use this little room to repair things, as we stored the soldering iron, spare bulbs, etc. in it. One night, a couple of my staff walked into the kit room and saw what they thought was me inside the cupboard with the door slid shut (it was still possible to see through a small gap where the door was not entirely flush with the wall). They also heard me in there moving things around. They assumed I was planning on playing a practical joke on them, jumping out and screaming 'BOO!' at the top of my voice. Deciding to prove to me that they knew I was there, but talking very loudly about how scary it would be if someone did jump out of the cupboard, they walked out joking that they were too scared to be in there. They walked out of the large doors of the kit room — and straight into me as I was coming in! They stood there opened mouthed, as I stood there slightly paranoid.

After explaining the situation to me, they turned back around and saw that the door had not moved, we had not heard anyone come out, and if someone had walked out of the room, I would have seen them as I facing in the correct direction. So we walked and slid the door back to find... no one there. The two staff members swore that they had definitely seen someone through the door and had heard a great deal of movement in there.

There were many more tales from members of staff and the general public alike, including floating heads, girls' voices, moving five-litre pots of paint, ladders that moved of their own accord and doors opening and closing by themselves. This continued for quite some time, but since they have become restaurants, the activities have died down a great deal.

Directly over the road from the old Megazone building, you will see what is now a collection of new buildings called Chelsea Square. As you look through the gate, you will see an older building, which used to be called Shaftesbury Hall and had a small theatre at the back of it.

The Theatre/Shaftesbury Hall (now known as Chelsea Square)

At one point, this collection of buildings used to be part of a college complex and included a theatre. Many years ago, I was a technician for a show that was going on in the theatre part of the building. As I was rigging up a light, I saw one of my colleagues walk across the stage area. I did not see him clearly, but as we were the only people in the building at the time, I assumed it had to be him. As I was speaking, I realised he did not reply, so I asked him a question again but this time louder. Unbeknown to me, he had just walked up the steps behind me, and he said, 'Alright no need to shout, I'm only here.'

Shaftesbury Hall

Now, this might not seem too paranormal. There was no way that my colleague could have travelled that distance that quickly, but it could have just been an intruder. When we got backstage, we decided it would be a good idea to check all the doors were locked and all the windows were closed, which they were. Then we went around the building trying to find who it was that was walking around.

We found no one — what a surprise — and all the doors and windows were closed and locked. Although we were not scared enough to leave, I did notice that neither of us left each other's field of vision for the rest of the day.

With your back to the gate, turn left and walk back up to the crossroads. Here, take a left and walk towards the church at the small roundabout. Before the church, you will see a small lane on your left.

Church Lane

A short tale of disappearing people now, told me by a friend about his friend (I never like these 'friend of a friend' stories, as it feels a bit like an urban myth then. I have had this verified though from another source). Anyway, his friend walked down this alleyway and saw someone coming towards him, so he moved out of the way. The figure walked past him and he thought nothing of it, but something was worming away at the

Church Lane

back of his mind, and seconds after this person walked past, he turned around to look at him — and couldn't see anybody. If you walk down this lane, you will see there are only a few places anyone could suddenly disappear — the occasional gate, or door — but my friend's friend was standing nowhere near these. He walked back down the lane trying to work out where the figure had gone but to no avail. Feel free to try and find him yourself, although people may start looking at you strangely if you keep walking up and down a lane looking for someone who is not there.

As you come back out of the lane, the same way you went into it, turn left and walk past the church and round the corner over the road from the side of the church. Here you will see what was a nightclub called Chemistry. Yet again, this is a story about a nightclub that has changed name, as Chemistry used to be called Gas.

Gas Nightclub

Years ago, a friend of mine used to work here, and she told me tales of a ghost who was rather annoying. Whenever she worked in the basement bar, she would place glasses down on the bar and walk away to get more, but when she returned the glasses would have been moved or would have vanished altogether. It took a while for her to realise that something was wrong. As most people do, she dismissed it as her working late and making mistakes, but then other staff started reporting the same things.

After a while, she started to accept that maybe something spooky was going on and she could no longer doubt it when she turned around to see a pint glass lift off the bar, float across it and then smash on the floor. She stopped working in the downstairs bar altogether after that and left her employment there soon after.

We have a bit of a walk now as you have to retrace your footsteps back to Yates's. When outside Yates's, cross the road and walk the length of the municipal offices (the large set of buildings that goes all the way down the road). Halfway along these offices you will find the entrance — if you want to go inside. If not, a bit further along you will find the tourist information office.

The Council Offices

Unfortunately, you will not be able to get into the haunted areas of the council offices, as the ghosts tend to frequent the top floor. I have spoken to many a past employee who told me of noises from the top floors, when they were supposed to be empty. Now, the good thing about this building is that, at the time of writing, it also houses the tourist information office, so head into there and see if they can give you any information on opening hours of any of the venues in this book.

Walk out of the building, and before you turn right, you will see the rear of a statue, a statue of another famous Cheltonian, Dr Edward Adrian Wilson (23 July 1872-29 March 1912). Dr Wilson was a notable English polar explorer, physician, naturalist, painter and ornithologist.

Gas nightclub

The County Council building

Turn right and walk down to the fountain. Stand behind the fountain with your back to it. The building in front of you is a relatively new building and before this one there once stood a cinema.

ABC Cinema/Neptune's Fountain

Unfortunately, the cinema building is gone, but it did have a story about a ghost that used to walk down the massive staircase that snaked along the wall of the building. Sadly, this staircase has now gone — and taken its ghost with it. Behind you is Neptune's fountain and quite often Neptune has his arm amputated: on several occasions it has been stolen or damaged and had to be replaced.

Now, if you walk around the front of the fountain and carefully cross at the lights, you are heading back to where we started at the town hall, and if you did not try the health-giving waters of the spa before, then now is your chance!

CHAPTER 2

GHOST WALK 2

Suffolk Arms

As always, it is best to start a long walk in a place of refreshment. In other words, how many pints can you drink before setting off on this hike? There are very few pubs in this country that do not boast a resident ghost and this one is certainly no exception. I have known many groups investigate this building over the years.

A lot of pubs talk about an eerie feeling in their cellars but then — let's face facts here — it is a room that is damp and often cold, with a very low ceiling and with strange noises from pumps going on — not exactly conducive to a lovely, relaxing feeling. I don't think many people will swap a holiday in the Maldives for such an adventure. Well, this basement is the home to a local rumour. Apparently, it is haunted by a girl who used to live in the cellar when the place was a hotel.

Many stories from this establishment follow the classic 'items being moved' format. Another thing that pubs that are haunted regularly report are the taps turning themselves on and off and — no surprise — that is alleged to happen in this pub too. Not only do taps turn on and off but strange tapping noises are also heard. Years ago, they even started to call the spirit the tapping maid. At a guess, I am assuming that she did not exactly give a superb performance with the ghost of Fred Astaire, more described the menu in Morse code. One story — which is somewhat stereotypical of ghost stories — tells of a member of staff hearing the tapping noises when she was down there. Assuming it was the landlady of the establishment, she went to talk to her only to discover she was actually on her own; not a soul was to be seen — well, not a living one anyway.

Walk out of the pub and turn left. Walk until you get to the traffic lights and turn left again along Bath Road. Walk for quite a distance, passing the pub on the right and taking the fourth road on the right. This is St Phillips Street.

St Phillips Street

You have now entered one of the most famous Cheltenham ghost sights, and one of the ghosts frequenting this area is well known because he was sighted by people who actually knew him when he was alive.

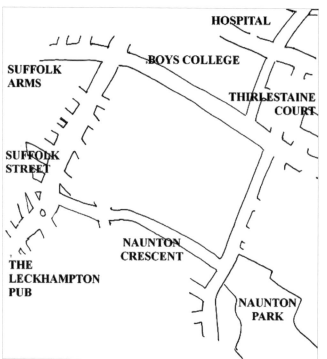

Left: Ghost Walk 2, part 1

Below: The Suffolk Arms

A public notice on St Phillips Street

You will find a small alleyway leading off St Phillips Street where many people have seen and heard strange things. One famous story is of a man walking down this alley. He moved out of the way to allow an elderly gentleman to pass, who then turned to him and said, 'I'm looking for my dog, have you seen him?' As the man replied in the negative, he heard a dog barking in the distance. 'There he is,' the old man said as he headed off in the direction of the dog's bark. As this figure walked away, the man remembered where he had seen him before. He was his neighbour — only he had died a few years earlier. He turned quickly, rather shaken, to see that the old man had gone. Another witness to the old man in the lane states that when they saw him he was carrying a gas mask and wore clothes certainly not of this generation.

Sometimes he actually manages to make it out of the lane and onto St Phillips Street itself. Now, if you want to see a ghost, this area is one of the most likely, as this ghost is seen in broad daylight.

There are many reports of this figure, who is often seen wearing clothing from the '30s or '40s and is often looking for a dog. So, if when you are stood here you hear a barking dog, then have a quick look around to see if you can see an old man, preferably one carrying a gas mask.

If you walk back onto Bath Road and turn right and then take the next right you will find yourself on Suffolk Street.

Suffolk Street

Bob Meredith tells a tale in his book, *Cheltenham Town of Shadows*, about a family who lived in Suffolk Street in the 1970s. During their stay here, they encountered several mysterious events. They even named one of their ghosts, which seems to be quite a common reaction to friendly resident spirits. This ghost was a young girl called Ada, she wore a brown dress and her long hair was tied back. She would stand at the foot of the stairs and would then walk through a blocked up doorway.

Another time, a member of the family saw her sat on the bottom steps of the staircase. Not really looking, they mistook her for one of the children in their family, and it was not until they got closer that they realised who it really was. At this point, the ghost of Ada disappeared.

She was spotted on another occasion and was also heard, as the step-father claims, crying in the attic rooms. These rooms were empty, and when the door to the attic was opened, the crying would cease.

Walk out of Suffolk Street onto the busy road that is Bath Road again; this time turn right and head towards the roundabout. The road branches off to the left, heading up towards Leckhampton Hill, or to the right, heading along the foot of the hills on Shurdington Road. I will not get you to walk down these roads, as the ghost story I am about to tell you happened in a building that has since been demolished. On the Shurdington Road you will hopefully see, a few hundred yards down on the right, a collection of new-looking houses, which were built on the sight of The Leckhampton pub.

The Leckhampton Pub

There is a well-known story of someone working behind the bar taking an order from someone, turning around, and when they turned back, the person had vanished. The bar staff checked to see where he could have gone but to no avail, they ran outside to see if he had left and could not see him outside either.

Immediately, you get the sceptics saying, 'Well, he must have walked out unnoticed or perhaps he had walked into the loos and no one saw him.' These critics and sceptics always think of an obvious answer and say that is what must have happened. Now, I know how infuriating that is, as I have often experienced these things first hand. People tend to tell me that I *must* be wrong. They then inevitably come up with a theory, satisfied that that is what happened. Never do they think that the person involved has probably already come up with this same theory — and checked it out.

So, if you really want to investigate ghosts from a sceptical point of view, then first ask the people involved and don't assume that what you think is correct. I am not saying that a ghost really did order drinks in this bar, but to be truly sceptical is also to be sceptical about the obvious.

Now, just before the roundabout on the other side of the road, you will see a road called Francis Street. Walk down this road, at the end of this road it turns into Naunton Crescent. Walk along this road as you read the next story (without bumping into anyone and then trying to sue me for suggesting reckless reading practices.)

Naunton Crescent

I have heard an interesting tale of a nurse ghost in Naunton Crescent. One young lady that lived on this road was very ill, and as she lay in bed, she used to see a black shadowy figure appear. Over time, this figure got closer to the bed and transformed into a woman in black wearing an apron. As the young lady got better and could walk around, the figure could be seen at the top of the stairs as she walked down them. Eventually, the young lady recovered and the ghost disappeared. Perhaps the NHS works even after death.

At the end of Naunton Crescent you will see a small park. This is the smaller section of Naunton Park. Cross this park to get into the larger section of the park. You will see a clump of trees on a small mound to your left and, way off into the distance, you will see an allotment.

Naunton Park

Reproduced here is an article published in the *Cheltenham Chronicle and Gloucestershire Graphic* on 9 July 1904:

The gateway to Naunton Park

The Hay Memorial Cottage Homes, Naunton Park, Cheltenham. In the spring of 1899 these cottage homes were commenced, through the generosity of the late Mr and Mrs Hay, for the benefit of the aged and deserving poor of both sexes.

The buildings are situated on a fine open site overlooking the Naunton Park Recreation Ground and commanding a good view of the Leckhampton Hills.

Two additional cottages (making twelve in all) and two wash-houses for the joint use of the occupants, have recently been occupied. This extension, together with the original buildings, was designed by Mr J Hall (who left Cheltenham last year, having been appointed Executive Engineer of Bombay), and has been erected according to the further drawings and under the supervision of Messrs Healing and Overbury, architects, of Cheltenham and Gloucester.

The outer walls are of Leckhampton stone, with 'chopped face', with brick lining; the roofs are covered with Broseley tiles; the whole of the half-timber work being in solid English oak.

The following inscription is carved on the oak beam over the ground floor windows of the central portion: 'These Cottage Homes were founded by John Alexander Hay and Marianne Louisa, his wife, AD 1899, as a memorial of their long residence in Cheltenham.'

The management of the homes is vested in the Mayor, Alderman and Rector of Cheltenham, and the total cost of the work, including site, has been nearly £3,000.

Mr Allen Wilson was the contractor for the main block of the buildings, and the extension has been added by Messrs A C Billings & sons Ltd of Cheltenham.

Look at that, a massive £3,000 spent on a row of cottages — you couldn't get them double glazed for that now. I just thought I would put that little clipping in the book to give you an idea of the age of the park.

Now, before you read the next section, try a little experiment. I want you to walk around the gardens and sports field and note down anything — any words that come to your mind, any feelings, any strange sights you see. I want to see if you get the same results that lots of investigators have achieved before you. Finished? Then read on.

We did an open-air investigation here a few years ago. Open-air investigations are always slightly awkward, as we can't control any of the external problems, such as noise, air currents, etc. We persevered and tried our best. On arrival at the site, Paul and myself did our usual sensory mapping (see end section for details on sensory mapping) and I came up with an image of a man, from a Civil War-type era, stood in the allotment area staring in at the field. We then walked around the park, and I felt a horrible sense of fear and trepidation as we came across the mound, a small collection of trees on a mound to the left of the park as you walk into the recreational sports ground area.

A friend of ours was recording a radio show about investigations and hauntings and turned up a few hours later, so we told him to try the same sensory mapping experiment. Interestingly, he experienced exactly the same feelings in exactly the same places: a Civil War-era figure staring in from the allotments and a sense of foreboding near the mound. Now, this is not exactly a small park, so to pick up on the same things in the same places was truly remarkable.

During the investigation, I was stood at the entrance of the park at about 11 p.m. and watched a misty figure appear and float towards me. Thankfully, it disappeared before it got to the gate, as I think I would not have coped too well if it had reached me. Our

Naunton Park mound

investigation did not produce too many other anomalous activities, and it was rather cold, so it's not as if our thermometers were going to show any amazing activity.

One story about the park features a rather noisy spirit. A group of investigators were in the park and heard a great deal of screaming, to the extent that the law was called in, but they found nothing. Now, one thing that most decent ghost hunters know about screaming or crying is that foxes can make some very disturbing noises. The emergency services say that ninety-nine percent of the time when they are called out to investigate a crying baby in the woods, or a screaming woman, it is a fox. Now these investigators were well aware of these noises and assure me that it was definitely human.

We have been given many stories of a rather scary nature involving this park and most of them involve the mound area. I would love to tell people all about them but they involve people that might not want their medical history written up in a book for all to see. I will say, though, that it ended in one person being hospitalised for his own mental health. I always say that no one has ever been harmed by a ghost, but be aware that if you are on the edge of a nervous breakdown then ghost hunting may not be the hobby for you.

Retrace your steps back to the Bath Road. Turn right and walk the length of the road, past all the shops, until you reach the junction with Thirlstaine Road and can see the boys' college in front of you.

Bath Road, with My Nan Outside the Boys' College

This is one story that I was not sure about including, but it is a good example of a psychic link causing an image to appear. My Nan was very ill and in hospital, and we were warned that she might not make it. I headed out one Saturday morning to the hospital to go and visit her, and as I got alongside the boys' college I 'saw' my Nan. It is hard to explain, but I have seen things that I know others are not seeing, and this nearly always turns out to be a ghost that is haunting a particular building or person. This was a similar experience, I knew nobody else could see her but about one hundred yards in front of me stood my Nan waving at me — then she was gone. Straight away I knew that it was too late and that she had died, five minutes before I would get to the hospital. I continued walking and bumped into my mum and her sister who told me they had just received a telephone call and that Nan had passed away.

These types of stories are very common, in the same way that people know who is on the other end of a telephone before it rings. The spiritualist will tell you this proves life after death, the more sceptical investigator will tell you that this only proves telepathy (the ability to communicate using just the mind), and the very sceptical investigator will tell you this proves I ate too many magic mushrooms for breakfast.

Turn right down Thirlstaine Road and keep walking as you read this next story. Make sure you stop when you get to the end of the boys' college sports green, as we are heading down the road called College Lawn.

The Boys' School

Thirlstaine Road

I will tell you to stop here, as I cannot give away the exact location of the next ghost because of someone's wishes of privacy. It happened a long time ago, but ghost hunters looking through your window asking if they can come into your house is never a fun prospect. Further down this road you will see a turning for Thirlstaine Court.

I will hand over to the *Gloucestershire Echo* to fill us in on some of the story.

12.12.1979 — *Gloucestershire Echo*
There were more odd happenings at Thirlstaine Court, Thirlstaine Rd, Cheltenham, yesterday — shortly before a Church of England clergyman went there to investigate a 'spooky' incident which happened last week.

Now, there are some fascinating reports of poltergeist activity in this building. It seems as though the building had changed hands and was now being renovated for the Gloucestershire Health Authority. One morning, a carpenter was alone in the house working, when a gas cylinder belonging to a portable lamp was torn from its fittings in one of the upper corridors. It was then hurled down the stairs by some unseen force, eventually landing in the hallway, which was twenty feet below. This, to say the least, was unexpected. The building firm then contacted the Bishop of Gloucester and it was agreed that they would exorcise the building.

Now, this ghost obviously liked gas, as a few days later some workmen were dismantling an upstairs pipe when it mysteriously ignited. Some people may think 'so what? That might not be too unusual'. However, the house had remained empty for the last eighteen months and the gas supply had been cut off a long time prior to this event. Once would have been bad enough, but this happened three times during the morning's work.

Before this building was owned by the Gloucestershire Health Authority, it had been a school for troublesome children, and a member of staff at the school said that the children were reluctant to enter or stay in any of the upstairs rooms unless accompanied by a teacher.

One of the most common manifestations of a haunting seems to be footsteps, and a teacher from this school reported hearing the heavy footsteps of someone walking up behind her when she was in the kitchen. When she turned around to confront the person, there was nobody there.

Turn left down College Lawn road and cross the road into Keynsham Road. Walk along this road until you get to the Lido and stand in their car park as you read the next stories.

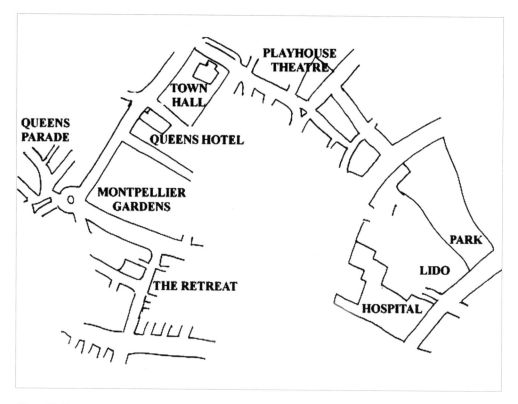

Ghost Walk 2, part 2

Keynsham Road

As is the case in Cheltenham, and lots of other cities, large buildings get broken up into flats. One of the flats on this road seems to still be the home of a lady dressed in black. She has been reported in a couple of the flats, sometimes wearing a white lace collar. She has the amazing ability to walk through walls and is aged somewhere between thirty and forty, or one hundred and thirty or forty — depending on if we are talking about the ghost's date of birth or how old she actually looks.

I am always fascinated by the fact that spiritualists tend to talk about spirits of children or older persons contacting their family. It seems rather unfair that if you die as a child you are stuck as a child in an afterlife, or if you were ninety when you died then you have to be ninety for eternity. Personally, I would like to be about twenty five, with all my hair and teeth intact — I wonder if you get to choose.

Another fascinating aspect of these types of ghost are the colours of their outfits; it would be nice if the lady in black appeared again, as that way we could see if she has faded at all, making the dress now grey or even white.

Lido

A colleague of mine told me a tale from when he worked at the Lido. Several of the staff became rather worked up when they came in one morning to find one of the gates unlocked. However, when reviewing the CCTV footage it showed the gate being

Sanford Lido

locked and checked. Ghosts then must have unlocked the gate and let themselves in — obviously they wanted to do a spot of midnight skinny dipping.

Other Lido tales tell of mysterious figures and strange feelings of not being alone in the ladies' changing area. The latter has been reported by a few of the female members of staff when they are closing up or on their own cleaning and tidying the place. I do not think they have ever found some peeping Tom running around the ladies' changing rooms who evades capture by making ghost noises.

If you are on a ghost walk in the middle of summer then perhaps you might want to go into the Lido and have a quick swim. The Lido, built in the 1930s, is an excellent building, which has survived pretty much still in its original form.

Originally the land was owned by Cheltenham College and was purchased by Cheltenham Borough Council for use as allotments in 1927.

In the early 1930s, there was a national movement to improve the nation's health. The first proposal was heard at a council meeting to suggest that the town would benefit greatly if they built a Lido. At the time, there were a great numbers of Lidos being built, especially in London.

It is astonishing that, back then, at a time of mass unemployment and poverty, so many local authorities were getting money for these altruistic projects. It is a shame that today, when we are in a similarly bad economic situation, large amounts of money are not pumped into these kinds of health-promoting projects.

If you are stood in the car park with your back to the Lido, then to your right you will see many buildings all connected with the excellent Cheltenham General Hospital.

Hospital

Now, any hospital will have a huge number of ghost stories attached to them; I have never failed to find a hospital with resident spooks.

I am very aware that ghost stories are quite a touchy and emotional subject, particularly when attached to buildings such as these. Therefore, I will not mention the names of specific wards or staff. I will also keep these tales down to just a few of the older stories, as you could write an entire book about the ghosts of hospitals.

One nurse told me of an intriguing ghost that likes to go for a ride. She told me that one time she saw a ghost that seemed to have a 1950s military feel to him. He was sat in the back of a car and turned around to look at her — only it then transpired that there was actually nobody in the car. I have since had this story confirmed by another nurse. She also told me of how many nurses seem to have seen the grey lady walking around the hospital.

My favourite concerns the mortuary. People working there have heard noises coming from the mortuary, and, most frightening of all, one worker looked up to see a figure stood outside his door, wearing a shroud and looking very pale and ghastly. When the figure moved away, the frightened man ran to the door — to see nothing but an empty corridor. So long as it was not medical students having fun, that has to be one of the scariest situations you could find yourself in.

There is a figure of a nurse that haunts one of the wards, that apparently frightened one of the patients so much that they were found trying to get out of the window. This may or may not be the same entity that managed to move the curtains around a bed on one ward. Anyone who has stayed in hospital knows that the beds are surrounded by curtains that can be pulled all the way around. One day, when all the other ones were perfectly still, one bed curtain started to whiz around the rails, with no visible means of propulsion.

There are many more stories about this building. However, you may be convalescing in hospital and a friend has bought you this book to cheer you up, so I don't want to be held responsible for making anyone petrified of the ward they are in!

Walk out of the Lido, turn left and then into and across the park. Cross at the traffic lights as you leave the park and then turn left. Carry on walking, with the park on your right, and follow the road around to the right. On the opposite side of the road, you will see a small road. Cross the road carefully and head downwards. You will come across a turning on your right, and a large building that used to be The Mitre pub stands in front of you.

The Mitre Pub

I have heard many stories of ghosts here when this used to be a pub. People apparently glimpsed figures from the corners of thier eyes — and when they turned around the figures had vanished. There are tales of poltergeist activity and strange noises in the night, but the scariest thing happened at the pub about ten years ago.

A colleague of mine was staying the night in one of the spare rooms. I would like it to be understood that she did not know of the ghost stories associated with The Mitre. She is also a level-headed woman and would probably not have believed the ghost stories, even if she had been told. Well, she was staying in one of the spare rooms. She had been in bed for an hour or so, lying awake on her side, but with her eyes closed. She said that it suddenly felt as though someone was next to her, and she went ice cold. She opened her eyes and saw a man lying next to her. The man, however, was see-through — the kind of thing we expect a ghost to look like. I asked for a description, but, like most people who have seen a ghost, she replied, 'I did not stay long enough to see what he looked like'; my friend ran straight out of the door and into a room with some 'real' people in.

Stand with your back to what used to be The Mitre pub. On your right, you will see St Luke's Hall, and on your left you will see a thin road. Take this road and you will come out near the Playhouse theatre

The Playhouse (see previous walk)
The Town Hall (see previous walk)

Walk out of the town hall and turn down an alleyway on the right of the building; this way you get to walk across the gardens and past the Gustav Holst statue. You will see a large white hotel on the other side of the gardens, and that is where we are heading now, as we stand outside the entrance.

The Queen's Hotel

My granddad told me stories, from people he knew that had worked there, of a figure that was seen often in the kitchens of the Queen's Hotel and how things would move around. This building has been remodelled and revamped several times since, and reports are rare now.

Walk past the Queen's Hotel, with the building on your left. After a hundred yards, you will see a way through the buildings over the road. Walk through this gap and turn left, with the church and the shopping centre on your right. At the end of this road, you will see Montpellier wine bar and over the road is a row of houses and flats called Queen's Parade; this next story happened in the first building of that row.

Queen's Parade

Many years ago, I lived in a dreadful little flat in one of these buildings. It was tiny and eventually, I think, the council closed it down as a slum, but I was a student and it was very cheap. One day, my brother, a friend and I were sat watching the television in my room, and as my friend turned away from the screen (he did not

Queen's Parade

see it, unfortunately) something large and black, about the size of a cat, but more like a shadow than a solid creature, jumped from behind my television to the floor. The thing then floated very quickly across the floor and under a small shelf in an alcove on my wall. My brother and I immediately stood on chairs and asked our friend to see if he could see what it was. Oh, how brave we were! Suffice to say there was no shadow cat hiding under a bookshelf — and no way for anything to have escaped either.

With your back to the wine bar, turn left and cross the road, where you will see a pub called the restoration. Cross over and stand with your back to this pub then turn left and follow the path around the end of the road. You should now be looking at a roundabout, and over the roundabout you will see a park on the left-hand side of the road and a row of houses on the other. This is Montpellier Terrace. Walk down this road until you reach the traffic lights.

Montpellier Terrace

This ghost story dates back at least as far December 1883, when it appeared in the publication *Merry England*.

View from Montpellier Terrace, *c.* 1830s

The start of the story is quite believable as ghost stories go. It follows a normal pattern: the house owners report strange noises, footsteps running up and down staircases, objects moving and voices talking in the room next to the room they are in. A ghostly figure is even reported to be seen and mistaken for a member of the family — until closer inspection.

Now, the later part of the story takes a bit more of a stretch of the imagination to believe. One of the sisters reported hearing noises from under her bed, so her and her sister took a look and saw what they described as black creatures, like toads but with horns and tails, come running out across the room and disappear through the skirting board. Now, I would say that this was nonsense, if it was not for the fact that, only a few hundred yards in the other direction, I had a strange black creature jump and run across the floor, only to disappear through the skirting board — but then people say I'm mad.

You should now be at the traffic lights. Cross here and head down the road and you will see Suffolk Parade opposite. Walk down this road and stop when you see a large church hall style building. Over the road is a pub called the Retreat.

The Retreat

The pub has a few stories attached to it, so it may be worth heading in, sitting down with a pint and asking if anything has happened recently. The ghosts seem to go from the pub into the flats next door. There is a small door next to the pub that leads up some stairs that have a rather eerie feeling. This feeling probably gets a little more scary when the shadowy figure is seen on the landing and going through a wall.

With your back to the Retreat pub, you can see a large church hall style building. This used to be a hall for groups to use and is now a restaurant.

Old Church Hall Building (now a Restaurant)

I was told these stories by two groups of investigators, both of which investigated this establishment a few times over several years. The conclusion of group one: the building is most definitely haunted. The conclusion of group two: the building is most definitely not haunted.

This illustrates perfectly that just because a paranormal investigation group know exactly what they are doing and have all the latest equipment, it does not mean that a ghost is going to turn up. Most of the time, a ghost hunt ends in absolutely nothing happening, which is exactly what you would expect. If every time a group went out they came back with fantastic results then I would be suspicious as to their honesty.

Years ago, I used to rehearse here with the Everyman Youth Theatre and occasionally I would hear noises coming from the stage area when there was nobody in the vicinity. Most of the stories, however, come from the other end of the building, near the staircase. These stories centre around a man who fell down the stairs to his death. As with all stories like this one, it is very hard to verify, and I have not found any evidence that

The Old St James Church Hall

someone did definitely die from falling down the stairs. However, that does not mean it has not happened.

Now, one group of investigators did an overnight vigil in the building and said they experienced absolutely nothing. On the other hand, another group were in there and said they kept hearing someone walk up the stairs when nobody was there and nothing else could have made the noises.

With your back against the Retreat turn left and walk down this road until you get to the main junction, passing a glorious building called the Daffodil on your left. It used to be a fantastic cinema, now it's a restaurant. As you get to the junction turn left and you will be only yards from the Suffolk Arms again. So take a well-deserved rest, put your feet up and order a pint.

CHAPTER 3

GHOST WALK 3

This walk ends up in Pittville park so you may want to make an afternoon of it and take a picnic with you. If you are reading this in the summer, then you may even want to play golf, as you end up at Pittville pitch and putt course.

The Brewery

The reason I am starting off in this complex is because this used to be a brewery and had many stories attached to it when it was the original building. The occasional figure has been spotted moving around here and, more interestingly, voices have been heard emanating from empty rooms. So, an interesting place, and one that I look forward to hearing more about over the years. Generally speaking, the ghosts are likely to attach themselves to the older parts of the building and the original brickwork. Therefore, we are going to set off on a rather nice walk through the Pittville and Fairview area, which is home to one of the most famous Cheltenham ghosts of all time, and then around Pittville Park. At the park you can see all the birds and animals kept near the playground, and you can even try the waters if you are lucky in the Pump Rooms.

Cross the road at the traffic lights at the rear of the complex, heading over the road to the car park, then turn right and follow the road around the corner. Opposite the car entrance of the car park you should see a little lane, Northfield Passage. Walk down this lane as you read this section. At the end of the lane, turn left and you should see Northfield Terrace.

Northfield Terrace

A recent story from this road involves a poltergeist. There have been reports of items moving around and strange knocking noises, both without any rational explanation. These reports are very recent and hopefully the poltergeist activity will evolve into something even more exciting; poltergeist hauntings always tend to start with subtle activity (normally knocking sounds) but usually progress into more obvious activity, such as unexplained voices and loud noises.

65

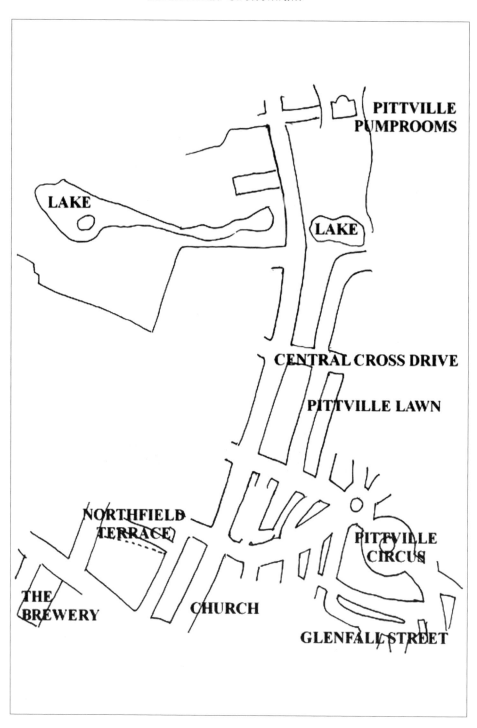

Ghost Walk 3

The Brewery

If you are lucky — or unlucky, depending on whether you want to see ghosts or not — then poltergeist activity becomes quite prolific, with unexplained phenomena such as objects becoming airborne. The thing to note with paranormal movement of objects is that they tend to move in a strange way. Instead of an item following a ballistic curve like a cannonball would in an arc, the angle falling away more rapidly at the end of the arc, the objects tend to move in a straight line and then fall directly down, with a ninety degree angle to the journey of the item.

We have also found that the smaller the item, the louder the noise it makes when it falls. Contrary to all rules of science, poltergeist activity throws out many questions that I won't attempt to answer. The myth that poltergeist activity always centres on teenage girls still seems to be prevalent; in our research, however, my team have found that poltergeist activity is just as likely to happen to a forty-year-old man as it is a fourteen-year-old girl.

Cross the large car park towards the church and turn left. Keep going until you get to the traffic lights, here you turn right and follow the road around, with the large green Pittville Park gates on your left. Follow the road round to the left, with the shops on your right-hand side. The second turning on your right is Albert Place.

Albert Place

I was told this story by one of our trusted investigators. He told me of a family who used to live on this street and had the fortune of listening to a musical ghost. The mother of the family and her two children all heard an old lady's singing coming from the basement of the house. The basement used to be the kitchens and bathroom of the house, so perhaps she was making them breakfast or running a bath for them, either way, I don't think I would partake of it myself. One of the children even saw the old lady. Unfortunately, I do not know what songs the ghost was singing.

As you walk down Albert Place you will see a turning on your left that you should take. As you head into Selkirk Street, you will see a turning on your right for Glenfall Street. Walk down Glenfall Street as you read the next story.

Glenfall Street

There is a second poltergeist on this road. A few years back, one of the houses on this street suffered from items falling off the shelves. I hasten to add that we are not talking about shoddy DIY and shelves from IKEA put up at weird angles but items lifting off the shelves and travelling across the room. At this residence, pictures were also reported as moving and coming off the walls. The front door would be heard to open and close and then footsteps walking up the short corridor to the lounge, which in this case was at the rear of the house. The footsteps would then stop, and when the door was opened, there would be nobody there.

These phantom footsteps also occurred when someone was in the shower, footsteps would come up to the bathroom and then stop, and when the frightened person eventually got the nerve to open the door, there would be nobody there.

Walk all the way to the end of Glenfall Street and come back out onto Selkirk Street. Next, turn right and you are on All Saints' Road. Turn left here and you will then see Pittville Circus Road turn off to the left.

Pittville Circus Road — The Cheltenham Ghost

This story holds a special place in our paranormal hearts — if you are a member of PARASOC — as it was investigated by the man we name our society after, Frederick W. Myers. We are named the Myers Society after him.

One of the most famous investigations of all paranormal history happened here in Cheltenham. When this was first investigated by the UK's Society for Psychical Research, SPR, it was called the Morton Case because it was the pseudonym the woman used.

There have been many articles and books written about the hauntings in this building, so I shall give you the brief history of the ghost. When the building was first built, it was called Garden Reach, later it became known as Donore and then the ill-fated St Anne's. It was first built in 1860 and bought by Henry Swinhoe shortly after his wife died. He did marry again; now, we don't know if his new wife drove him to it, but he became an alcoholic after this. The second wife, Imogen Hutchins, also fell

St Anne's

prey to the demon drink. Subsequently, they led rather turbulent lives, with many a quarrel. One of these quarrels was over jewellery. When Henry's first wife died, he had a small recess built underneath the floorboards of the front sitting room in which he placed his first wife's jewellery as a legacy for his children. Imogen, on the other hand, insisted that he gave the jewellery to her, a request he continually refused. Imogen left him before he died in 1876, yet she soon followed his departure and died herself in the year 1878.

In 1880, the house was then let to a man called Captain Despard, who lived there with his family over the next ten years or so. Despard had a daughter called Rose or Rosina. She first saw the ghost in June. She was by no means the only person to see her, and very soon sixteen other people, family, staff and friends, also saw her. The apparition was tall, dressed in the clothing of a recent widow and her face was obscured by a handkerchief. Rose wrote about the hauntings:

> The figure was that of a tall lady, dressed in black of a soft woollen material... The face was hidden in a handkerchief held in the right hand... on further occasions... I saw the upper part of the left side of the forehead, and a little of the hair above. Her left hand was nearly hidden by her sleeve and a fold in her dress. As she held it down, a portion of a widow's cuff was visible on both wrists, so that the whole impression was that of a lady in widow's weeds...

Apparently, she appeared as solid as any living human being to the witnesses and they mistook her for a real person. She had a regular pattern of visitation, as she would descend the stairs, stand by the sofa for a bit, then go down a hall to the door leading to the garden and disappear. One day, two of Rose's sisters saw her in the garden. Rose must have been an intrepid paranormal investigator herself, as she tried to communicate with the phantom verbally and using sign language.

The first time that she tried, she thought the ghost was going to answer, but it seemed as though she only gasped. As is often the case, not all the members of the family could see the phantom. I myself have been in a room with many investigators and only half the people present could see an apparition. Even though not all of the family members were able to see the phantom, they could hear the footsteps. Rose even tried to photograph the ghost, and she would place various strings across the halls and doorways of the house in an attempt to see if the ghost would walk through them without breaking them.

It is reported that once she formed a ring of people around the apparition in an attempt to try to catch her. The result was not fantastic, as she just walked between two people and disappeared. After 1886, the apparition for some reason was seen as often and seemed to fade slowly. This is not unusual, as phantoms tend to have a peak period and then fade away. (One famous haunting tells of a woman in a red dress, and over the years, this dress became pink and then white, and then all you could hear were the footsteps as she ran across the courtyard. This gave rise to a theory that ghosts tend to fade away over time and with exposure, like a photograph left out in the sun.)

Many witnesses all reported seeing this same figure over and over again, at all times of day and night and for up to half an hour at a time before she disappeared. If only video cameras had existed then, I would be a very happy ghost buster. She was also seen by residents who lived across the road, as she walked in front of the house in broad daylight.

It is thought that animals react well to psychic phenomena. The family dog, a Skye Terrier, reacted to the presence. It went to the bottom of the stairs and wagged its tail, as if in greeting. Suddenly, the reaction turned to one of terror. It slunk away, tail between its legs and hid under a sofa. However, the family cat showed no fear and seemed to be unaware of the entity.

The London-based SPR is one of the oldest parapsychological organisations in the world. Psychologist and highly respected Cheltonian parapsychologist F. W. H. Myers was one of its founders, and it was he who did the investigation. He heard about the ghost in 1894 and visited with the Despards early in the following year. It was Myers who suggested Rose try to photograph the ghost. Rose used the alias R. C. Morton when she wrote about the ghost for the SPR's journal, *Proceedings*.

It was believed that the ghost was that of Imogen, based on her height and known habits. The Despards moved from the house in 1893. It was vacant until it became a boys' prep school in 1898. During this time, the apparition was often encountered. The school closed and the house was vacant until 1901 when it became a nunnery. They only stayed for two years. The house changed hands several times, including when it was rented by the Diocesan Council as a conference centre and a retreat from 1935 until 1948. It was later bought by them, and they added a chapel in 1962. The house was closed and then sold for private redevelopment in 1973. When the house was turned into apartments, it is reported that tenants did not stay long and there were long stretches of time that it was vacant. One couple who stayed there shortly after it was converted stated that they had spoken to the workmen who converted their flat and both of them had seen the figure of Imogen coming down from the front steps. They then went on to tell their tale in full.

It was a Boxing Day night — no, this is not the sequel to *A Christmas Carol* — and the husband of the couple was returning home at about 10 p.m. On the main, well-lit staircase, he saw what he clamed to be Imogen Swinhoe. Unlike the earlier sightings, which all talked of her being dressed in widows' black, this apparition was dressed in grey, giving rise to the fading ghost theory once more. They spoke of all the other things that generally go with hauntings, objects moving and reappearing elsewhere, strange draughts, things falling from shelves, and they even spoke about paintings that flew off the walls and across the room.

Another tenant spoke of ghostly figures that he saw; he was leaving his flat due to a fire alarm practice, and looked up the staircase to see two old ladies on the stairs who then promptly disappeared.

There are more recent sightings of the figure outside of the building as well. One woman even had her driving test interrupted. As she approached the house, suddenly a tall black figure appeared ahead of her and stepped off the kerb. She did an emergency stop, so as not to hit her, but the figure just disappeared — as did her driving licence probably, as the driving instructor said that he had seen nothing. A postman also nearly ran over the phantom one morning as he was cycling along, she suddenly appeared in front of him causing him to swerve before she disappeared.

It is possible that this ghost has claimed at least one life. I always say there aren't any reputable reports of anyone being harmed by a ghost, and the only time people get hurt by ghosts is when they run out of a room screaming and fall down the stairs. This life taken was not human, but that of a dog. In 1979, a woman, her husband and a small dog lived in a bungalow very close to the house. They returned home to find the dog lying motionless on the floor; apparently he had had a minor heart attack. The vet seemed to think that it may have been connected. A ghostly attack or, more likely, the overactive mind of a vet?

Turn around and head back, but this time head towards the large green roundabout called Pittville Circus. Over that roundabout and the next smaller one, with a fantastic castellated building on your left, and you should come to Pittville Park. If you stand at the corner of the park, to your right you will see a road called Pittville Lawn and to your left you will see another road called Pittville Lawn. Take the left-hand road for about fifty yards until you see Weston House. Turn back around and walk along the edge of the park, heading towards the lake.

Pittville Lawn, Weston House

Now, Pittville has quite a long, grisly history. Before it was the park back in the 1700s, it was the Common, or the Marsh, as it was also known. The land was crossed by Gallows Lane, which ran all the way out to Prestbury. The bodies of hanged criminals were exhibited in gibbets here as well. Now, they were not built too well, and one, containing the body of Joseph Armstrong who poisoned his employer, collapsed back in 1777.

There are also two witches who were possibly buried in this marshy land. They apparently lived by some form of supernatural protection racket, and they would ask for hand-outs from their neighbours, all of whom were too scared to say 'no'. These were the self-same neighbours who refused the 'witches' a Christian burial when they died and instead buried them in the marshy grounds outside of Cheltenham.

This has a history of haunting going back quite a few years, with hauntings being noted before 1930, when there were reports of poltergeist activity that included heavy furniture being dragged around, notably in the upstairs rooms. This was also accompanied by a female figure — not that the female figure had ever been seen hurling furniture around. Most poltergeist activity takes place out of sight; you rarely see a ghost pushing a sofa and saying, 'Can you give us a hand, it's pretty heavy when you have no actually physical form'. I would have to admit to being pretty impressed if it happened; so until we see the death of one of the Chuckle Brothers, a ghostly 'to me, to you' is unlikely.

Back to the matter in hand. When the house became the centre of a medical practice in the 1960s, reports of noises from the upper rooms started along with the rustling of paper and a general feeling of unease.

Keep walking uphill across the parks until you get to a rather impressive temple-style building: the Pump Rooms. Once a place where you could partake of those lovely health-giving waters, the Pump Rooms is now a function room and sometimes an exhibition centre, with many a concert and recital taking place. It is well worth walking into the Pump Rooms and having a look around.

Weston House

The Pump Rooms

So, here is the tourist bit. The Pump Rooms was built by the architect John Forbes between 1825 and 1830. It is a Grade I listed building, which stands at the northern end of Pittville Lawn and has landscaped grounds running down to a lake. The building contains the original pump, made of marble, to which the waters are today fed by electric pumping. So, if you have missed out on the fantastic Cheltenham waters earlier then here may be your chance!

The building has a colonnade of Ionic columns, and inside, there is a ballroom on its ground floor. Further Ionic columns support a gallery under a dome from a time when domes were used to amplify live music. On the upper floors, there was a billiard room, library and reading room. Above the colonnade are three statues, which were erected in 1827 by Lucius Gahagen. The statues are of the goddess Hygieia, Aesculapius and Hippocrates.

If you walk out of the main entrance of the Pump Rooms, you will see a road in front of you. To the left of this road is a house that we were once called out to for a private investigation. For the sake of the people who live in the house, I will not tell you the exact location.

Private House (Just off Pittville Park)

We were called to investigate a building in one of the roads just off to the side of the Pump Rooms. As per usual with these private cases, we got called in more to reassure the residents that they are not going mad than to find a ghost. Most of these visits start with the home owners saying things like, 'you must think me stupid' or 'most people think I'm mad'. Believe me, it is highly unlikely that you will say something that we have not heard before. Having said all that, this is quite a rare case.

One of the occupants of the building tells how she was in the kitchen when a large black shadow, which she describes as looking like a large swarm of black bees, lunged towards her and then disappeared. We have heard of these formations before but they are very rare. Another regular visitor was an older woman who appeared in the garden, mostly in one spot, looking into the house.

When we did our sensory mapping experiment, the main thing we sensed was a figure standing in the garden staring in, and, as the occupants of the house later told us, the place we sensed the figure was exact location in which it had been seen. This goes to prove that you can have an investigation that provides no physical evidence and yet is still not a waste of time.

At this point, let me advise you to go for a walk around the lake. If you don't want to walk too far then I would miss this bit out. Hopefully, you have brought some bread with you for the ducks.

Pittville Pump Rooms

Pittville Lake

Pittville Lake, the White Lady

There is a tale of a ghost that wanders around the lake. She appears as a white figure floating along, sometimes over the lake and sometimes to the side of it.

One explanation could be mist rising off the lake forming into pockets and air currents, giving the appearance of an upright figure. Remember, the brain immediately tries to put everything it sees into categories, and if it sees something of vaguely human size and shape it assumes it is a human. Then, when the mist dissipates, the brain gets confused and may start thinking along the lines of ghosts to try and explain what it saw. Or is there really a ghost that hovers around this lake?

Possibly an explanation for our ghostly female friend here is that it is one of the Cheltenham witches, as mentioned earlier. However, there is also a story of a young woman killing herself by drowning in the lake. She was heading towards the hospital and feared that she was going to be diagnosed with cancer and, as the story goes, decided to kill herself rather than go through a lot of suffering. Apparently, the post mortem did not discover any cancer, and it is reported that this spirit has been seen, even by members of her own family.

If you have taken this walk and need to head back to Cheltenham, follow the road that dissects the two main areas of the park (Evesham Road) all the way back into the centre of town.

CHAPTER 4

GHOST WALK NO. 4

Prestbury, Medium Walk

Prestbury dates all the way back to the ninth century. It used to be a separate village from Cheltenham and it belonged to the Bishop of Hereford. When it was granted a market in the middle of the thirteenth century, it became a thriving market town on the route from Winchcombe to Gloucester.

The village of Prestbury became part of the Cheltenham Borough back in 1991, following a boundary change. It has a population of about 5,300. Prestbury has retained much of its olde-worlde charm and village character, with its collection of attractive houses, thatched cottages, pubs, timber-framed buildings and Cotswold-stone-tiled roofs. It gives the impression of Cotswold country village life — but also that you wouldn't see change from a million pounds if you tried to buy a house here.

It is surrounded by Cleeve Hill and contains a lovely medieval church, St Mary's, dating all the way back to the twelfth century. The area of Prestbury known as The Burgage is the place where the old market was, and this secluded area of the village hasn't changed much and houses quite a few of our spirits.

The Jockey (Opposite the King's Arms)

It was Gold Cup night in the 1970s. (It's hard to believe but some of you may not realise that Cheltenham is very famous for horse racing because the Gold Cup is held at the Cheltenham racecourse every year.) There were four women standing just outside the King's Arms when they saw a man wearing what looked like a jockey's outfit. Now, even though it was race week it was still an unusual sight. What made it even stranger was that, when the man walked across the road, he disappeared. This was startling enough, yet when they walked around the corner, they saw the whole thing happen again!

Stories like the above are my favourite type of ghost stories, as they have more than one eyewitness to corroborate them.

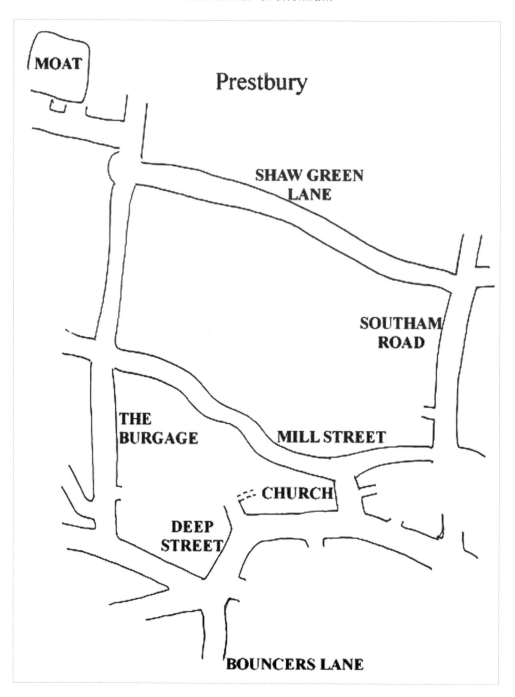

Ghost Walk 4

The King's Arms

Leave the pub and safely cross the road, heading for the old building that is the newsagent's.

Poltergeist in the Old Post Office (now a Newsagent's)

There was a woman who went by the name of Peggy Mayhew. She lived at the old post office as a child. She gave a fantastical description of how a poltergeist would move things around and hide items many times a week. Her brother joined her by testing the poltergeist. They were paranormal scientists at such a young age. They would place items at the back of shelves, yet the next morning they would be on the floor. (I am assuming that they did not have dodgy shelves built at strange angles.)

If you stand with your back to the shop, turn right and walk up the road, look out for a small turning on the right-hand side. You will see a street sign with 'Anne Goodrich Close' written on it.

The old post office

The old butcher's shop

Old Lady Peering into Windows (Ann Goodrich Close)

These Almshouses were built in 1720. A little old lady has been seen, on several occasions, dressed in non-contemporary clothes. She is often caught peering into the windows of the buildings all around the area. This has to be quite a scary apparition as, let's face it, anyone looking through your window is scary enough, so when they then simply disappear it's probably more frightening than the acting on Hollyoaks.

Keep walking along the road until you come to the butcher's on the right-hand side of the road.

Poltergeist in the Old Butcher's (the High Street)

The previous owner of this shop — it was a butcher's as well back then — reported various periods of poltergeist activity. He claimed items were removed from a storeroom only to be found placed in a pile in the middle of the shop floor.

There was also reported, on several occasions, a shadowy figure gliding around the room upstairs, and the shop owners heard whistling and sighing noises whilst they were working in the cutting room and office.

This was confirmed when we visited the shop to investigate. Two gentlemen were in there who had worked on the premises for quite some time. They informed us that when they worked out the back or upstairs, the previous owner, if he wanted them in the shop, would whistle to them. They would then dutifully stop whatever they were doing and head down to the shop floor to see a rather bemused shop owner asking what they wanted. We were told that this happened on many occasions and that they remembered the sighing noises as well. The gentlemen working in the butcher's seemed to think it might possibly be to do with a woman who met a grisly end there who, as often seems the case, with the spirit of some sad suicide victim, was returning because she needed some sausages — well, even ghosts like a barbeque now and again.

Opposite the butcher's shop, you will see a little monument and to the left of it Idsall House, tucked away behind the trees but still visible from the gate.

Apparition (Idsall House)

There is a spooky tale to tell of this building according to the *Gloucestershire Echo*, published on 4 March 1989. When this building was being refurbished, a worker, who was renovating the basement, tells of how he was pushed in the back — the strange thing being that no one else was in the room at the time.

A former resident of the house also tells of paranormal happenings. Apparently, she did not like entering the room at the top of the house in case she met up with what she described as 'the apparition'.

With your back to Idsall House turn right and walk to the end of the road; you should now be on Mill Street. Turn left and walk towards the pub that looks out onto the graveyard.

Idsall House

The Plough Inn

Horses' Hooves (The Plough Inn)

Whilst researching ghosts of Prestbury, the local Scouts seem to have posted many ghost stories online, so I thank them for this one and a few more of the Prestbury stories.

Years ago, a local postman by the name of George Hudson Dove often used to hear the sound of horses' hooves behind him at the Plough Inn. So it looks like if, you want to spot these ghosts, then it's an early morning for you. He would pull over to up against the church wall to let the horses pass, the sound would then cease and there would be no horses there.

It is also said that herdsmen find it difficult getting their sheep past the Plough Inn, and dogs and horses have been known to freeze to the spot outside it. So it looks like the best bit of ghost hunting equipment you can take here is a dog or some sheep. If you are lucky, then you will also see the ghost of the white lady as she walks down Mill Street and into the church graveyard.

Carry on in the direction you were walking along Mill Street.

The Marching Men (Mill Street)

The Mill Street area seems to be famous for ghosts that are a little shy, in that they seem to like making noise but not actually appearing.

There was a man walking his dog one evening through the fog along Mill Street when he heard the sound of marching men approaching. The dog seemed to become afraid and sank to its haunches, at which point, the sound abruptly stopped. However, no men appeared at all. This odd happening has been experienced a few times.

One interesting thing to note here is the weather aspect of the story. Many ghost stories revolve around the same weather patterns. If it was raining then the ghost appears again in the rain, and if it was a sunny day then it has to be a sunny day for the phantom to appear again. Some theories would agree with this, using the 'stone tape' theory. The idea is that it is a 'video' that has somehow been caught in the atmosphere, so if you replicate the conditions, you replicate the 'picture'.

The Charging Horseman (Mill Street)

During the English Civil War, a royal dispatch rider was riding from Sudeley Castle to Gloucester. Unfortunately for him, the Roundheads of Prestbury seemed to have taken a leaf out of Wiley Coyote's book and stretched a rope across the road that knocked the Cavalier rider off his horse. The rather unlucky rider was then put to death. The executed rider can sometimes be seen in outline form, along with the sound of a horse's hooves. A friend of mine has witnessed this on a few occasions but was not too willing to sit there with me trying to record it. I obviously thought he was too scared and accused him of a lack of back bone, but his reply was 'No, it's boring innit' — fair enough, I thought; I guess I am the equivalent of a paranormal trainspotter.

Mrs Preece's Ghost (Mill Street)

On researching Prestbury ghosts, I found one called Mrs Preece's ghost. I have yet to find out who this Mrs Preece was and why she would come back to haunt us, so any information would be lovely — feel free to email me. This apparition has been described as a white misty figure that floats across the fields — that is until reaching the wall. Here, the figure seems to pause before finally vanishing.

The Stick Lady

Bob Meredith wrote a superb little book about the ghosts of Cheltenham and the Cotswolds, which is still available today. In it he tells the tale of an old woman. She is often seen gathering sticks and passing in front of the windows of a cottage.

This is possibly an example of a ghost exhibiting 'stone tape' behaviour, which means that the entity itself is not interacting with its surroundings but rather is repeating an action over and over again, as though a video tape is continually replaying its image. The figure walks along the same path that probably ran close to where the cottage is now. Quite often, these apparitions disappear when challenged in any way or if you put something in their way — the theory being that you are then interfering

The Burgage

with the picture and, just like a television aerial, the interference causes the picture to break up.

You will now be standing at the junction that brings you to a ghostly hotspot, that of the Burgage. Turn left onto the Burgage and walk along the pavement whilst admiring the historic cottages and buildings.

The Medieval Messenger (the Burgage)

Now, it seems as though horse-mounted messengers in this area are not liked that much, as a medieval messenger was galloping down Shaw Green Lane on 4 May 1471 when he was struck in the chest by a single arrow.

His spirit, on a phantom white horse, is another of Prestbury's famous phantoms, and he is often seen riding around this area before suddenly vanishing. Perhaps he is racing the other horse-riding messenger, which eventually leads to the world-famous Cheltenham races and they built a race course near the site to commemorate such a famous phantom — or perhaps I should just stick to the facts!

One of the more grisly facts concerns the early part of the twentieth century. Workmen, whilst carrying out road repairs, found a skeleton that had an arrowhead firmly stuck between its ribs. Now, at a guess I would assume this is the same person, unless Prestbury has a serial killer with a penchant for horse riders and a love of Robin Hood stories.

The Girl Playing a Spinet (Sundial Cottage, the Burgage)

Now, I am a musician, but I don't think I have ever heard anyone play the instrument that is the spinet. The case of Sundial Cottage, therefore, would have been one that I would have loved to have investigated. The end of the nineteenth century saw a peculiar case of a young girl being seen on several occasions playing a small piano-type instrument called a spinet in the garden of Sundial Cottage. I am always interested in apparitions that appear outside, as most people tell of shadowy figures in dark corners, but ghosts that appear in normal daytime sunlight are much more fascinating.

Now, it has rarely been reported that anyone has seen this figure for the last hundred years but it is still possible, occasionally, to hear the music emanating from her ghostly instrument. One interesting story tells of a mother and children who moved here during the Second World War to escape the Blitz. The children kept saying they were afraid of the funny music that played at night-time in their room. Their mother, probably thinking this was all nonsense, swapped rooms — only to be kept awake by the phantom music herself.

Sundial Cottage

The Young Girl and the Sound of Horses (Prestbury House Hotel)

A lot of hotels used to try to deny that they had any ghosts, as it could sometimes be bad for business; it is only recently that hotels have started boasting about their ghosts in the hope of attracting some ghost-hunting tourism. For years, whenever we asked the Prestbury House Hotel if they had any ghosts, they would deny any stories. However, local people talked of a young girl who has been seen in the gardens of the hotel. They would also tell of the sound of horses' hooves in front of the building when no horses were present.

Previous employees have talked of a room that was so active with psychic phenomena that they had to stop using it, so instead it was either boarded up or used as a storeroom.

As you reach the end of the road, you will see a house opposite you with a large gate and surrounded by trees. This is Walnut Cottage, recognisable by the pub-style signpost at the gate.

86

Prestbury House Hotel

Old Moses (Walnut Cottage)

This story is from the marvellous ghost walk that the Prestbury Scouts have published. A previous resident of the cottage by the name of Mrs Campbell invited a certain Mr and Mrs Sharp to tea. Mr Sharp was a smoker and had accidentally left his pipe in the dining room. He walked back in there to see a man stood by the fireplace, who turned to him and said, 'My name is Moses, I like to look in on her sometimes.' Mr Campbell later found out that there used to be a character named Moses who did odd jobs in the village.

If you are stood with your back to the gate, then cross the road and turn right until you reach the corner with the roundabouts. To your left, raised slightly from street level, you will see the Vicarage.

The Vicarage

A friend of mine once lived in the Vicarage, as his father was a vicar in Prestbury — I won't say which one, as we try to make sure people stay anonymous. He told me that he had previously, on a few occasions, woken up to find a figure at the end of the bed — a figure that was not his wife, I hasten to add. He has also seen the Black Abbot, on numerous occasions, around the village and in the church as well.

Follow the road around the corner and you will see a row of small, stone cottages.

Row of Cottages

As you walk along this road (Deep Street) you will see a row of three old cottages on your left. The last time I was walking along here I noticed that two of them were up for sale, so now is your chance to live in a real haunted house!

There are tales of a ghost with the X factor along here. When I went on a ghost walk many years ago I was told of a ghost that liked to sing. Her voice could be heard emanating from one of the cottages, yet nobody in them was singing at the time.

One of these cottages used to be the vicarage, and the church had the building exorcised. I am not sure who won the battle, the X factor or the eXorcist factor, as I have not heard tales of a singing ghost for a while.

Deep Street

The ghost may be wanting to stand in the spotlight, and strange lights have been seen glowing from inside one of these cottages as well.

At the end of these cottages, you will see, tucked away at the back, a small white building called Reform Cottage.

The Black Abbot (Reform Cottage)

Now, this building has a fantastically haunted past, which features many an apparition. Quite rightly so, as apparently the front garden was once a burial ground of monks — always a good selling point for an estate agent, I find — and not only that but home to Prestbury's most famous resident, the Black Abbot. Apparently he was a regular visitor to the cottage.

When Mr and Mrs Couzens moved in, they did not know it was haunted and they did not believe in ghosts, but soon they regularly heard footsteps outside, often followed by bumping around upstairs. A lot of the time, noisy ghosts are ignored for quite a while, as people put noises down to traffic or floorboards creaking, but ghosts can haunt a building for years before anyone puts two and two together and realises that actually 'no, nobody in the family does play the piano in the living room and, more importantly, we do not own a piano'.

When Mr Couzens passed away, Mrs Couzens sold the house to a man from London by the name of Ian Highley. Ian and his wife planned to move in but first

Reform Cottage

they were going to make alterations. They had workers in to make the alternations upstairs, and this is when the activity picked up; many builders will tell you stories of hauntings, and it seems that when you start disturbing a building it unlocks its secrets. After the alterations were made, Mr Highley and the workmen were all inspecting what had been achieved when all of a sudden a pot plant that was suspended from one of the beams began to swing violently from side to side. This pot plant then freed itself from its hook and hurled itself across the room, smashing onto the floor not far from where the men stood. Unfortunately, my sources do not tell me if they continued to stand there or ran screaming — like most of us would — from the premises, never to return.

You can follow this road until the bend, but instead of following the road around to the right you will see a smaller way in front of you that leads to a lane, which leads into the church graveyard.

The Black Abbot (St Mary's Church)

The most famous ghostly inhabitant of Prestbury has to be the Black Abbot, who is seen many times throughout the year and by many people, villagers and travellers alike.

St Mary's Church, Prestbury

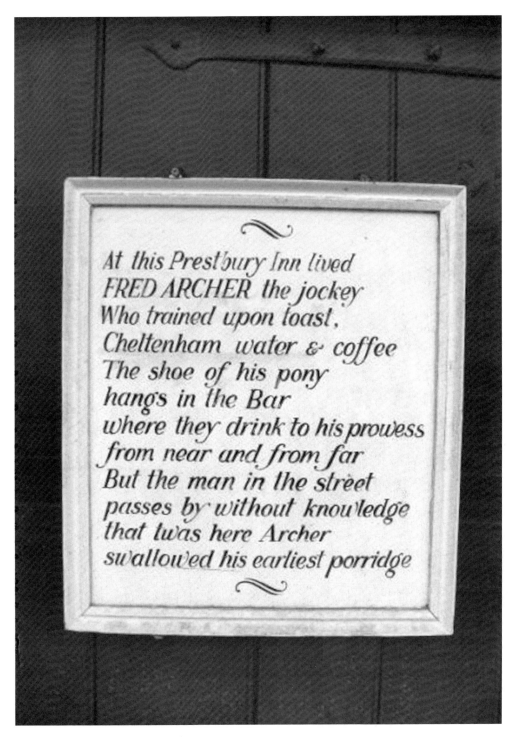

At this Prestbury Inn lived
FRED ARCHER the jockey
Who trained upon toast,
Cheltenham water & coffee
The shoe of his pony
hangs in the Bar
where they drink to his prowess
from near and from far
But the man in the street
passes by without knowledge
that twas here Archer
swallowed his earliest porridge

Plaque on the King's Arms Inn

He was often to be found in much older times walking down the aisle and naves of the church, that is until the church was exorcised, at which point the Black Abbot moved into the churchyard and village. Not so much an exorcism as an exclusion zone order. If you want to stand a chance of seeing this ghost then the best times are at Easter, Christmas and All Saints' Day but sometimes after a funeral as well. The hooded figure, with his head bowed, seems to always be described as appearing to glide rather than walk.

His route seems to be similar each time he is seen, and with any luck, not only will you be on a ghost walk, but you will also see a ghost on his own little walk. Starting from the church, he crosses the churchyard and heads towards the old priory. Here he enters the grounds of Reform Cottage on the main street. His route can vary and sometimes he is seen walking in the direction of 'The Bishop's Palace', a mated enclosure which seems likely to have been the Bishop of Hereford's hunting lodge. I have even heard of him on the main High Street and known of people having to swerve cars and bikes to avoid him.

To the right of the church, you can walk back out onto the High Street and finish where we started at the King's Arms pub.

The King's Arms

This place contains some of the best spirits you will ever see or, more importantly, drink. I would recommend finishing your ghost walk sat in a comfy chair with a glass of scotch to steady the nerves — and hopefully you will be visited by the ghost known as Fred.

Previous managers who have lived on the premises tell of how they lock up the entire building, and when they come back, they see doors and windows open, which can only be opened from the inside.

If you are sat in the pub, listen out to see if you can hear people upstairs when there is no one in the building, which is a common occurrence.

Keep an eye open for the shadowy figure that walks near the restaurant entrance. The cleaners have often seen this figure when they are working and the pub is closed with only them in it. The kitchens have many a report of unusual happenings, and one of the previous chefs often saw the ghost of the old lady on the High Street when they looked out of the windows.

Definitely keep looking out of the window, as you may spot the Black Abbot; he has been seen very often on the High Street and once or twice by people in the pub.

CHAPTER 5

GHOST WALK 5

Prestbury

Follow the previous walk, but after Idsall House, turn right along Mill Street and head towards Southam Road.

A Funeral Procession (Southam Road)

Now, ghosts, with their associations with death, are grisly enough but what about a ghost story about a funeral procession? A local teacher was returning home one day through Prestbury, and as she was driving along Southam Road, she saw a funeral procession that was crossing the field towards her. This was a rather unusual sight to see — the black horses and mourners walking along — so, rather confused, she turned the car back around to get another look, only to find... nothing. The funeral procession had completely disappeared.

If you look along the road you will see the corner where it joins with Prestbury High Street again. You do not need to walk down here as we will double back on ourselves.

A young motorcyclist was coming from Southam down Cleve Hill and onto the High Street when he saw a woman dressed in clothing not of the time and wearing a mob cap. The apparition walked out and went across the road — or should I say through the road, as she appeared to be a foot or two below the road's surface. The motorcyclist braked so hard to avoid hitting the woman that he was thrown from his bike and suffered cuts and bruises down his leg.

Turn left. We are heading out of Prestbury towards Southam. This is quite a long walk, so be careful along the major road. You will pass, on your left, Shaw Green Lane (take note, as we will return here soon). Be warned, as this is quite bit of a trek for one venue — one to save for a bright sunny day.

Hotel de la Bere

The story goes that a nanny, who worked here when it was a establishment of education for young ladies, hanged herself here in her bedroom. She still roams the corridors, apparently making sure that her charges are all in bed asleep.

On leaving the hotel, we return again and head up to the crossroads, where we turn onto Shaw Green Lane.

Shaw Green Lane

The fields inbetween the Shaw Green Lane area and Mill Street are home to many strange noises, so as you walk along here, try to do so quietly and listen out for phantoms. If you are lucky, then you might hear the sound of marching troops and men on horseback. Marching is normally heard moving towards the Mill Street direction and into Prestbury.

After Shaw Green Lane, turn left onto the Burgage. Follow this road until you see Mill Street on the left, you may wish to walk down Mill Street to find out all the stories as you return to the previous walk.

The Vicarage

At this junction, reports coming from the 1970s onwards tell of a headless horseman. He is seen as a full apparition or as a vague misty outline, but he is always mounted on a horse. Whether this is one of the killed horsemen from the Burgage now looking for his head we don't know.

After the Vicarage, you will be at the junction of Deep Street, Blacksmiths Lane, Bouncers Lane and Prestbury Road, very carefully head across this junction and down Bouncers Lane. Keep walking until you see all the allotments on your left.

Bouncers Lane Allotments

It is possible that you are doing this ghost walk in the dark, late at night, as this is definitely the best time to see this reported spectre. Look carefully at the allotments and see if you can see a glowing figure. Very often it is reported that this figure is bending over, possibly even gardening — maybe it is harvesting pumpkins for Hallowe'en.

Turn back around and head towards the junction again and return to the previous walk.

When you finish this walk, relax in the King's Arms and read a few more stories about Prestbury.

Cleeve Corner

A house that is near Cleeve Corner has a ghost that likes a spot of strangling, so if you're feeling slightly choked then you may have encountered this unfriendly spirit. Some say it is the ghost of a woman who was strangled in one of the houses there.

The High Street

One of the houses along this road, seems to be haunted by an apparition who likes her headwear. This is a little old lady, always seen walking around in a large hat. She walks from the kitchen to the bedroom and then disappears.

The Hanging Man

One of our researchers tells a tale of something that happened to a few acquaintances of his. A group of young men were walking through Prestbury and headed off across a field in the direction of the racecourse. They soon discovered a rather grisly sight: a man hanging from a rope by his neck in a tree. They ran away rather scared, but as soon as their composure was regained, they turned around to see... nothing there. However, all of them had definitely seen the hanging man only seconds before.

CHAPTER 6

OTHER CHELTENHAM GHOSTS

Honeybourne Railway Line

This railway line has since become a cycle path, so feel free to walk along it, but as you do, spare a thought for its previous residents, as not only did the town have to rehouse hundreds of people to build this line but it also had to dig up 300 bodies from the town cemetery that was once here. Perhaps it is one or two of these deceased residents that have returned to their final resting place when shadowy figures are seen and then disappear on this eerily quiet cycle way.

Queens Parade, Montpellier — the Dark Shadow

My brother and I were sat in a top floor apartment of one of the Georgian buildings on Queens Parade. we sat quietly watching television, when a shadowy shape about the size of a cat jumped down from behind the television and ran under some shelves in the corner of the room. Now, when this happened I was student with very little money, and the room I was in was very small, there was nowhere this thing was to have disappeared, and thankfully a friend of ours happened to be in the kitchen. We summoned him into the room, with instructions to look under the shelves, he walked in to find these two intrepid ghost busters stood on chairs pointing to the corner saying, 'It went over there'.

Suffice it to say there was nothing there, and it went down in history as NOT my best ghost-hunting moment.

The Beaufort Arms

An acquaintance of mine was telling me of a haunting that seemed to affect only one person. The person in question, who worked at the Beaufort Arms, used to get poked and pushed by some form of spirit. He thought this was weird enough but soon got used to it. Well, one day, the aforementioned gentleman got up and walked out of the bar to go to the toilet. Whilst he was gone, my friend and a few others watched this man's pint move along the bar, then slide around the corner of the bar and move towards them.

This part of the story particularly interested me. Often PARASOC are given stories of moving glasses in pubs and you have to treat them with some scepticism: the bar may be on a slight slope or uneven or wet, all of which could lead to moving glasses. However, this glass, we are told, not only moved but also changed direction and went around a corner, following the curve of the bar, stopping in front of the witnesses.

When they gentlemen returned they informed him that his glass was now near them, adding that none of them were willing to touch it.

The Fox and Hounds, Prestbury

Like most pubs, this one has a chequered history. It contains what is possibly the spirit of a previous landlord who hanged himself. There are reports of unexplained noises, and there have been sightings of this ghost.

Coniston Road, Hatherley

Not long ago, the *Gloucestershire Echo* did an article on me because I was writing this book, and, as so often happens, they asked the question, 'So how did you get started in the ghost-hunting world?' I often have standard answers to this type of question. This depends, however, on whether I am on TV, where anything over a two second answer is deemed too long, or on the radio, where the local DJ is really only interested in hearing his own voice, or the local newspapers, where they are going to misquote you anyway.

So one of my answers is as follows. Many years ago, when I was living at my parents' house, my younger brother came into my room and said that there was a strange flapping noise in his bedroom. It sounded as though there was a bird or bat flapping its wings around our head but there was nothing in the room. We then went into the attic to see if we could see anything above the room; there was nothing in the attic. The noise, however, continued.

Whenever you tell stories like this one, the people reading them will automatically jump to conclusions and assume that it was a bird or bat, although obviously we thoroughly checked that possibility. The strange flapping sounds seemed to occur more and more over the next few months. When we mentioned this to our older brother, who had previously occupied that room, he said, 'Oh yeah, that happens all the time.' He was never one to be amazed by the supernatural. Our parents still — at this point, anyway — thought we were in need of medical assistance and possibly a visit from some nice men wearing white coats.

Another encounter with this invisible little beastie happened in the kitchen, and this time, we could hear it walking around our feet as well. This incident was witnessed by my brother and I and a few other independent witnesses who knew nothing of the flapping ghostie upstairs. Now, we only had a small house, so opening a zoo of ghosties was not an option here.

My parents still seemed to think I was insane (not an opinion that seems to have changed); then my father heard it. He describes it as something that sounds like it had a twelve-inch wing span of leathery wings. He was sat in the front room reading, when from behind the TV unit, he heard the flapping. He described it by saying that he was half expecting something like a gargoyle from a horror film to come flapping out from behind the television. This happened a few times, until he decided enough was enough and left the room. Now, to all you sceptics, there was not a bat/bird/small woodland creature/over-active imagination running around the house.

Whatever it was, it seems to have left my family in peace since. Just like our tortoise, which ran away (it turned up a year later two gardens away — it wasn't a very fast runner), our ghost menagerie has moved on.

Another story I have from this residence is all about the lights in my bedroom. I came home one day and put my key in the lock. It was the middle of winter, so it was dark very early. As I turned the lock, the lights in my bedroom went off. I knew that the doors were all locked, so I started to panic that there was a burglar in there. Grabbing the nearest weapon, I set out to examine the house. I stopped in my tracks very quickly when I realised the nearest weapon was a broom, so this was quickly swapped for a carving knife. I headed out into the unknown or, even, upstairs. I must admit, I was scared more because, halfway up the stairs, I realised I was carrying a very large knife and had no idea what I was going to do with it if I did bump into a burglar. I went all over the house and, thankfully, found no one.

This lighting problem happened a few more times before I moved from there, so either a ghost who does not like the light or dodgy wiring — you decide.

Colesbourne Road, Benhall

This rather stereotypical ghost story involves the ghost of a little girl, and I was told recently that three out of four of the people who lived in this house saw this ghost. Our informant told us of how she was sat one day in her lounge and a young girl appeared next to her and ran out of the room. I always find these stories interesting — the ones where the ghost runs out of the room — as I love to think of someone, rather scared, sat in the room thinking they can't get out because their only means of escape is blocked by a ghost!

The Odeon Cinema

Previous employees often tell me tales, particularly about screen five. One ex-employee told me that she was cleaning up in the cinema when no one else was around and a malteser sweet came rolling along towards her. She didn't think too much of it, as the floor was littered with popcorn, sweets and drinks. It was not until the second one rolled towards her that she started to panic, as this time it was rolling uphill. By the time the third one was rolling, she was out of the door.

Glencairn Park Road — a Flat in a Large House

Yet again, this is the story of an annoying poltergeist. I lived in a little attic flat in one of the buildings on Glencairn Park Road. We were often visited by an annoyingly playful poltergeist who liked to hide objects. The sceptical investigator would, at this point, think 'Well, you just misplaced the objects and forgot where you put them'. So, I will relate a story that makes that explantion seem most unlikely. We had rented a DVD from a rental store for the night and we took it home and placed the disc in the DVD player; then, as always, we put the DVD case on top of the DVD player. The next day, I went to take the DVD back but found that it was not in the player, not in the case and, after about two hours searching, I also established that it was not in the flat. Being a man, I assumed it was somewhere obvious in front of my eyes and that I just needed some woman to come along, call me an idiot and find it in about ten seconds. This, however was not to be. When my girlfriend returned, we both ransacked the entire house but it was not to be found. The next day, when we awoke, we walked into the front room to find it there on the floor with nothing around it; it would have been impossible to miss the day before.

This poltergeist had a habit of leaving things on the same spot, and one day we heard a metallic thudding noise and turned around to see my house keys lying on the carpet in the middle of the floor. I know that no one ever believes this type of story until something similar happens to them; in this instance, everyone will assume that it must have been me misplacing things. However, when I started looking into these events, I was amazed at how many people have had similar experiences. Well, there are simple ways of testing this and that is to take photographs of your house every day, so if something seems to have moved then you can go back and check if it really has.

CHAPTER 7
PARASOC INVESTIGATIONS

A Cheltenham Church

I do have to be slightly sensitive about this investigation, as churches do not like to talk about hauntings and this involve, someone who died not too long ago. I will change the names of the people, and ghosts, involved.

A friend of mine, let's call him Bob, used several rooms of a church to rehearse music in. He let himself in using the keys, so therefore he knew that the building had previously been locked. On walking up the stairs, he, and another performer, saw a girl dancing at the top of them. They were obviously rather bemused, as they had only just unlocked the building and this girl must have been locked inside all night — not to mention the fact that she was dancing. 'Bob' confronted her and asked her what she was doing there, to which she replied, 'My name is Mary.' The figure then disappeared before their very eyes. A few days later, they were in the graveyard when they saw a relatively recent grave; the grave was of a girl of the same age as the dancing apparition — and with exactly the same name.

St Georges Road

A friend of mine called us in to investigate his top-floor flat at an old house on St Georges Road. He no longer lives there, so we cannot print his address — that would be rather unfair on the people who live there now. To give you a vague idea of where it is though, it was around the area where the road is at its highest.

He told us that he was lying in bed one night when he saw something very small glowing and floating around in his hallway. He thought, as any rational human would, that he was being confronted with something unusual, perhaps something a little like a firefly. He had never seen a firefly and this seemed the most rational explanation, but then the glowing light came into his bedroom, got larger — it was now within a few feet of the bed that he was lying in — expanded, turned into an image of a little girl, and then ran through the doors of the wardrobe and disappeared. He was suitably shaken at this point, and not long afterwards, he called us in to investigate.

This property gave us some fantastic examples of annoying ghost behaviour. On the first investigation, we walked in and started to set up all our equipment. We placed a tripod with a night-vision camera on it in the corner of the room. After doing this, we decided to take a photo of the room (this is done in case something subtle has happened that you were too engrossed in the investigation to notice). My favourite camera for this part of an investigation used to be a Polaroid camera, as these are instant and therefore cannot be messed around with to create fake images. I have later found, however, that this is not the case and fantastic 'ghost' images can be made by pushing chemicals around an image before it develops.

When I took this photo there were several people in the room; we all heard the noise, so we turned around to the camera to see a shoe box had moved across the room and wedged itself on its end underneath the tripod. Therefore, unfortunately, the only paranormal phenomenon we captured was the reaction of four people on camera all staring and saying, 'Did you see that?' This tends to be the case, as ghosts are notoriously camera shy, and if there are five cameras in the room, then you can guarantee the ghost will appear in the one bit of the room not covered by them.

Now, as a group, we do not do anything like Ouija boards or séances, as they tend to give such subjective evidence that it tends to be useless. However, as this guy was a friend of mine and thought it would be fun, we said we would join in if he wanted to do one. Thankfully, we had it all on camera, so we could play it back to him to prove that Ouija boards tend to be rubbish — just the people in the room pushing a glass around subconsciously due to ideomotor movements and muscle spasm in the finger tips. I could talk for hours on the subject of their pointlessness but, suffice to say, we thought it would be funny. Whilst we were doing this Ouija board, and getting various results, including a supposed spirit that liked my friend's record collection and was particularly partial to Jazz, the video camera, which had been quite happily sat on a flat surface for the last hour, decided to jump to the floor (and when night-vision cameras cost hundreds of pounds, this is not a paranormal manifestation you want to happen too often).

We played back the footage, and just before the camera fell to the floor, we saw small orbs of light flying out from under the table. The camera had to move about four inches to the left before it could fall off the surface.

Orbs

Some people think that a thing called an orb is the first manifestation of a spirit, so let me explain a little about orbs. Orbs tend to appear on digital cameras — not just digital cameras, but most of the time, this is where you will find them. If you search through your own photographs then you will probably find one or two, at least.

They are balls of varying sizes and are sometimes a brilliant white colour, sometimes a soft grey and barely visible. Most of the time (in fact, virtually all of the time), these can be explained away as photographic anomalies and defects in the technology.

Where orbs become interesting is when they exhibit a form of intelligence behind their movement. If the orb can be seen with the naked eye then this is by far the best type, as it obviously cannot be explained away using the standard explanations. I will illustrate this using one of the cases that we examined as PARASOC.

We were investigating a pub, or should I say had been invited along on someone else's investigation. We often get called along as 'experts' in the field, because we tend to be quite scientific and also rather sceptical about most claims. The groups more

Orbs at the Playhouse. Some say pictures of spirits, others say just dust

on the 'believer' side of paranormal research like us to come along and lend them some form of credibility. Be warned that we do not do this as standard practice, and some groups have not liked it when we have come along and explained away all their supposed phenomena by discovering leaking pipes, dodgy sealant on windows and lights reflecting from car headlights.

During the investigation, Emma was fortunate enough to be in a room with her night-vision camera. She caught two orbs performing on camera, and the best thing about this footage is that she also filmed and recorded an interesting soundtrack. On the film we see other people in the room pointing to the orbs, proving that they were visible to the eye. We also have the audio recording of them all saying where the orbs were moving to. Emma also states that she could see these orbs as bright lights flying around the room.

Now, the truly sceptical reader will now by laughing out loud and proclaiming that we are all insane and obviously they were faked torches, reflections, lasers — whatever you wish to use as your standard method of explanation. One thing you must remember, however, is that a true sceptic who refuses to believe anything is just as guilty of self-deception as one who believes in everything. You cannot have an open mind if you have already closed it to all possibilities.

So, I do not wish to go on and on about the methods we use when I explain each case — it would not make an interesting read for you, the lovely people who have spent your hard-earned cash on this book (and hopefully on the sequel). Suffice to say that, of

Fellow ghost hunters Emma and Paul from PARASOC

course, we investigated every possible reason for the lights and failed to come up with any satisfactory explanation that was not paranormal. We always try to replicate the phenomena whenever possible to see if it is at all humanly fakeable. On this occasion, it most definitely was not.

The better images and footage tend to be called BOLs or balls of lights, as the word 'orb' can tend to get some negative responses even before you have shown the evidence. I am always interested in orb footage, so if you manage to get any really good footage, then please send it us on the PARASOC website, www.parasoc.org.

Malvern Road

I cannot divulge the actual address of this house as the occupant has left now, and I don't think the present occupiers would like to be unnerved if they have not seen or experienced anything themselves. We also say that we guarantee personal anonymity unless the householders wish to go public.

I was called up late one night by a fantastic ghost hunter, the rather eccentric yet encyclopaedically knowledgeable C. J. Romer. A man who has more ghost hunting hours under his belt then anyone I know, C. J. Romer has worked on many TV and radio shows about the paranormal, and, yes, that includes being a researcher at various points for the Living channel's scream-fest that is *Most Haunted*. He called me to say that he had been contacted about a case and could I get there as soon as possible. It was only around the corner for me, so even though it was nearly midnight, I jumped on my bike and headed out.

When I got there, C. J. had managed to call up a few other ghost busters and we walked in. At this point, the only person who knew anything about what was going on was C. J., so we decided to do the sensory mapping and wander round filming a few people saying what they think may have happened.

If you have read any of the other paranormal series books, you may have come across Lyn Cinderley's book *Paranormal Gloucester*. I mention this because she often calls me a medium in her book because I am often capable of sensing previous events that have taken place in haunted houses. Actually, though, I tend to think of myself as a sceptical ghost hunter and, besides, I am definitely an extra large and not a medium.

As I was walking around being filmed, I came up with an image of someone stood at the bottom of the stairs, a male, and then a small female who seemed to come from the back of the house on the first floor and into the bedroom to show somebody something. Another one of our intrepid ghost hunters had a go, without hearing what I had said, and started to talk about a young female that would appear in the bedroom at the front of the house; unbeknown to each other, we seemed to have come up with the same stories.

As we were invited into the house to try and calm down the woman who lived there, having two strangers walk in and identify the apparitions that she had also seen was not too helpful. She had seen the young girl in her bedroom and also spoke of her child talking about a man at the bottom of the stairs. We did not experience any actual paranormal behaviour that night, but there was definitely a good score on the sensory mapping front.

The Eagle Tower, Bath Road

Well, the name of the building makes it sound as though it should be some gothic haunted castle on a bleak moorland somewhere, but in reality it is pretty much Cheltenham's only skyscraper. That makes it sound more impressive than it really is, as it is not exactly massive. It's more of a cloud tickler than a sky scraper. It used to be the home of Eagle Star insurance, and that explains the large Golden Eagle statue on the Bath Road side of the building. It is a rather impressive statue and I think they may have realised that it was better to change the name of the building to 'Eagle Tower' when the insurance company left than to have to try and explain why there was a large glittering bird of prey sat outside.

Now obviously the building is not very old in historical terms. We are not talking a Tudor beamed coaching lodge or Georgian health spa, but it does have a bit of a murky history. The story goes that whilst under construction in the 1960s there was a mortality. One of the construction workers fell to his death down an empty lift shaft. The young

Above, left: Paul and Bruce from PARASOC taking readings before an investigation

Left: Bruce on an investigation, in night-vision

man seems to have affected the one hundred and fifty foot lift shaft ever since, as the lift that he met his fate in seems to go up and down of its own accord, even though there is nobody in it. The security guards report this happening even when the building is empty so that they know that nobody has pressed a button on another floor. I expressed my doubt at this story as lifts do occasionally do this, yet on further inspection these lifts are not designed to do this and have been checked on several occasions and had no fault found with them.

The lifts I guess would be unnerving if you were stuck in them on your own, and suddenly the doors open to reveal no one, and it must be extremely infuriating for security guards who have to check it out each time, just in case it is a lazy burglar who can't be bothered to use the stairs. The security guards however are not the only people to report strange phenomena, as the cleaners have had their share of frights as well. We are told that many times during the evenings when cleaning shift workers are alone in the building they see objects moving and doors opening and closing of their own accord. I have not been able to speak to the cleaners who experienced this so I cannot verify the tale myself yet whilst talking to various ex employees they all confirmed these stories. They also tell of an unexplained chill that would take over the reception area in particular, and cold spots that would suddenly drop in temperature throughout the offices.

Now one interesting aspect of the story is CCTV. Many people say that ghosts can not be captured on film, which then leads to all sort of allegations of lying, or hallucinations. Mark Williams, a security guard in the building, tells a tale of how his colleague John Dyed had a security camera pointing at the foyer. When he ran the footage back, it showed an apparition walking across the floor, and then disappearing through a wall at the far end. Now, unfortunately, I have just been handed this story so as the book goes to print I have not been able to track down the recording, so let's hope there is a *Paranormal Cheltenham 2* with updates on previous stories.

Mark himself says that he has heard the spirits, and during one of his late night patrols, he claims that he was coming out of one lift and heard voices in the lift next door to his own. When the door opened surprise, surprise…. There was no one there. Suffice it to say he was rather scared. As all good ghost spotters know you end up actually liking the ghosts though and would be upset if they left. Yet on a cold dark winter's night it can still be very scary so I finish this story with a few words from Mark,

"I am used to it now, but it was scary when I started."

The Cotswold Inn, Portland Street

Well my ghost hunting group has a particular affiliation with this establishment, and not just because we all like a pint or two, but because this is where we meet up every month, so I guess it was inevitable that the talk would turn to ghosts within the building itself.

There is a figure that is seen in the cellar area of the building, and has moved a few things around whilst down there. Now none of this was told to us before we did an investigation in the cellar area. We turned up and as per usual Paul got out a night vision camera and filmed me as I walked around and did a sensory mapping experiment, I did not seem to get a huge amount but felt like there was a figure in the cellar where the beer was stored, we plotted this onto a map and then let someone else have a go, three people did the experiment and came up with exactly the same results. Not one of us spoke to each other about our findings, and each person had a different cameraman who also knew nothing of the whereabouts of the spooks. We did not get any other interesting results that evening except for a banging noise from the same area that we all mentioned, but then the pub was open upstairs, and it may have been some noise that happens from time to time when pints are being poured in the bar above us.

So this is the perfect example of an investigation where seemingly nothing happened yet we managed to get some correlating evidence, to support the fact that a certain area may be haunted. With investigations like these our next task is to go back and see if there is a reason why people would feel a certain way in a certain area, and try and rule out any natural causes. More importantly we shall return as we have our meetings there, and they do a particularly good scrumpy cider.

Shurdington Road

Along Shurdington Road there are various industrial estates and warehouses, as well as a haunted hotel which I cannot write about yet as we are going to investigate hopefully very soon. It is the long road that stretches all the way along the bottom of Leckhampton and Crickley Hill, and finishes off at the foot of the cheese rolling hill. Now for those of you who do not know about the cheese rollers it is a strange custom we have here in Gloucestershire. Once a year we hurl large cheeses down a hill and, what some would class as idiots, run down it and try and catch the things. Most people end up falling and rolling, or to put it more correctly 'bouncing' down the hill into the arms of the waiting

St. John's ambulance brigade who try and patch them up again. Once patched up these strange courageous individuals decide they want to do it again and clamber back to the top of the hill.

Cheese rolling is classed as the world's second most dangerous sport, and I am sure if you tried guessing then you are unlikely to guess the number one dangerous sport, as apparently it is cheerleading. You are more likely to suffer injury from cheerleading than any other activity, so if you are watching the cheese rolling do not start cheering for anyone as it could be fatal.

Anyway to escape from this digression, I will tell you of the warehouse that we investigated along this road. I can't tell you exactly where or which building it is, as they asked to be left anonymous. We sent a small team of investigators to go along and check out the building, to draw floor plans and take the large amount of readings we like to have before we start our investigation properly. The building consists of one very large room used as the main warehouse, a large empty office on the first floor, and on the ground floor under the office area, a toilet, the entrance hall, and storage cupboards. We decided when we got there that we may as well have a go at sensory mapping, so out came the night vision camera, and Paul started filming me as I walked around saying whatever gibberish came into my head. It turned out that I managed to pick up on a couple of areas of interest, yet I did not seem to come up with anything concrete at all.

Whilst we were filming though we heard some banging noises coming from the office area on the first floor. Paul and I thought it must be Bruce moving things around, yet when we came to the end of the shelving unit we saw Bruce stood in front of us. We all heard the noises and went upstairs to investigate, but there was no one there. This investigation was rather late at night and we knew that all the surrounding buildings were empty, there were no cars parked outside, and if anyone had got in they would have needed to be a key holder, as we locked up as we walked in.

We went downstairs whilst Bruce was upstairs trying to recreate the noise, now this was rather difficult as the office was empty, except for one cupboard, a chair, a kettle and some mugs there was very little to bang around. Bruce jumped up and down, and hit walls, but it was not until he started to bang the cupboard against the wall that we recognised the sound. It was exactly the same. The only noise we could come up with was a cupboard moving of its own accord and banging on a wall.

Unfortunately the next time we investigated, we did not get any strange anomalous behaviour at all. We were then told the stories about the place, which included strange noises but also things moving around, which just so happened to correspond to the areas we picked out on the sensory mapping.

Investigations like these are ongoing, and we tell people that if strange events occur then to write it all down, so if anything like this is happening to you make sure you copy the report sheets and investigation techniques in this book, and please contact us to come along and investigate for you. I look forward to seeing you and your ghosts very soon.

One of the leading scientific paranormal investigation groups is based in Gloucestershire So if you think you have any unexplained phenomena, we may have the experience to explain it for you.

www.parasoc.org

Science is catching up with superstition,
more and more strange goings on like ghosts, poltergeists,
or even spooky noises in the night can be explained
with conventional rational methods

Yet there are still a few that cant

So if you are experiencing ghosts, objects moving, unusual
smells, lights or noises, or anything you think you can't
explain, we might be able to help you

We are not
SPIRITUALISTS,
MEDIUMS,
or even
GHOSTBUSTERS

We are a group of investigators using science to explain the
unknown. With a proven track record explaining and
recording paranormal activity in the country's theatres,
pubs, clubs, private homes, and even prisons

Our members are often used as advisors for TV, Film,
and Radio and treat each case with the utmost
respect and privacy

just visit

www.parasoc.org

to contact us

CHAPTER 8

HOW TO BE A GHOST HUNTER

This last section of the book is all about how to be a ghost hunter and be taken seriously. Let's face facts: anyone can wander round a house saying, 'is there anybody there?' If something amazing actually happened, then you have to have some form of credibility and this is the reason I suggest you do not touch Ouija boards and don't go in for dowsing or séances. I will not say that they are all rubbish and you must be mad if you believe in them but I will say that other people will definitely think that.

If the only evidence you have for the case is that you came up with names and dates through a Ouija board, regardless of how correct those facts are, 90 per cent of the scientific community will not listen to what you have to say, and the general public will think you are messing with things you should not mess around with.

Equipment

Below is a list of recommended equipment you should take with you to an investigation. Obviously, some of these items are quite specialised or expensive so don't panic if you can't get all of them. All you really need for an investigation are some eyes, ears, and pen and paper, but if you really want to get seriously into this as a hobby, then this is a particularly good list to start you off.

Air Ion Counters
This piece of equipment is designed to measure positive and negative ions in the air. It is thought that paranormal activity causes a large number of positive ions because it gives off high amounts of electromagnetic discharge.

Audio Monitors (such as Baby Monitors)
These allow you to remotely listen to any activity taking place in a particular room. You can now purchase baby monitors with video feed as well, and eBay is a fantastic resource for buying cheap broadcasting cameras.

Bags and Cases (for Security)
When on an investigation, we would recommend that all equipment not currently being used is stored out of sight. The main reason for this is that you will most probably be

using expensive cameras or camcorders and therefore wouldn't want them to get stolen. The other reason is that if you keep all your leads, cables and other equipment in a bag or case, then it will prevent people from falling over them. The large silver box-style photographer's/DJ's cases are ideal, and they are relatively inexpensive and sturdy enough to stop damages if dropped.

Barometers
Some investigators believe that paranormal activity can also have an effect on barometric pressure.

Batteries
These are an essential item as paranormal activity is thought to have a direct effect on electromagnetic fields, which can cause batteries to go dead or to run down quite quickly. Remember that in a cold environment batteries can lose their charge, so try to keep them stored at a constant temperature. Digital cameras are also very power hungry and will wear down batteries very quickly. We would recommend that you take twice as many batteries as you think you may need, as they can drain very quickly if paranormal happenings occur.

Camcorders
Although not always the cheapest piece of equipment, a camcorder is almost an essential in today's paranormal investigations. There are literally hundreds to choose from, Hi8, mini DV, digital, etc. It is always best to get the most for your money, so it's a good idea to shop around for the best price — they differ greatly! Yet again, eBay can prove to be an invaluable tool here, but remember that if the price seems too good to be true, then it probably is.

Candles, Matches and Other Emergency Lights
These are important items just in case your touch and equipment stop working. Remember to be careful where you use an open flame, especially in historic locations! It is best to get permission for using candles from the property owner just to ensure there are no issues (their insurance may prohibit a naked flame on the premises). Candles can also be used as good indicators of draughts in a building.

Clothing
It may sound obvious, but England isn't best known for its sunny weather, and outdoor locations can get a little muddy! Coats and wellies, therefore, may not be the height of fashion but they are extremely useful.

Compass
One use for the compass is to help identify unusual electromagnetic forces. If you are a beginner and cannot afford lots of equipment, this is an ideal (and cheap!) alternative to an EMF Meter (but you won't get as many results). Most outdoor sports stockists (Black's, Millets, etc.) will have these. The main reason we use compasses is to ensure that, when taking readings, our equipment always faces the same direction.

35mm Cameras

If you cannot afford a decent digital camera, then this is the next best thing. In fact, many paranormal experts will tell you it is actually better to use a 35mm camera (preferably an SLR) than a digital camera. This is because a digital camera has no negative, which is required by third parties to verify that a photograph that purports to show paranormal phenomena has not been faked. Make sure you remove the camera strap, as so many photographs turn out to be straps out of focus due to their proximity to the lens. Also, try to avoid taking pictures in inclement weather when outside (many 'orbs' are just light refracting off condensation) and try to refrain from smoking and exhaling breath in cold conditions. Make sure you take the film to the best developer in your area and always tell them to print all the photos, even if it appears that there is a problem with a couple of them (they won't be looking for paranormal activity, and most places do not develop photographs that have issues with them). We recommend you buy the best camera your budget will allow.

Digital Cameras

A digital camera is a very useful tool for capturing any pictures as they enable you to view the picture immediately, and you can even analyse further if you have a laptop with you. This will ensure you are aware of any paranormal activity that is not seen by the naked eye. It is best to get a consensus of opinion on what you think you can see in a digital photo, especially with orbs or smoke-like apparitions, which can normally be easily explained.

Digital Recorders

These are very useful and are quickly becoming the item of choice for obtaining EVPs, electronic voice phenomena. There are various types used but the most popular tend to be recordable MiniDisc or a Dictaphone. The information recorded can be downloaded to a PC for further analysis of the sound waves (if you can afford that type of software!).

Dowsing Rods

Some investigators feel that dowsing rods can be used to pick up and locate paranormal activity and ghosts. However, it is very difficult to prove any results you may find and many people will disregard this type of evidence.

Dowsing Pendulum or Crystals

Similar to dowsing rods, some investigators feel that pendulums and crystals can be used to pick up and locate paranormal activity and ghosts as well as being a tool to communicate with the spirits. The same issues as with dowsing rods arise with pendulums or crystals, so if you use this type of equipment, then try to get information that can be cross-referenced and proven.

EMF Detectors

These detectors are designed to identify fluctuations in electronic fields over different frequencies. We generally use these to determine the level and strength of electromagnetic fields in a location.

First Aid Kit

It is always useful to have a first aid kit with you on an investigation, especially if you are outdoors, just in case an accident arises.

Food and Drink

We would recommend that alcohol is never drunk whilst on an investigation as no one will trust your results. Make sure you take enough drink with you, especially essential if outside where you will not be able to buy anything. If taking food, try not to eat smelly or noisy food (as a large amount of paranormal activity, especially in poltergeist cases, revolves around smells and sounds).

Infrared Thermal Scanners

These devices are designed to identify where cold spots are but they can also record changes in room temperature. The price varies greatly and is dependent on the quality.

Laptop Computers

An expensive item to have but a laptop is very useful when using a digital camera. The laptop will allow you to download images immediately for ease of viewing and analysis. If you have a webcam, then the laptop can also be used as another video camera. The extensive use of a laptop on an investigation varies greatly, depending on the software you use.

MiniDisc Recorders

Very useful, both for recording your investigation 'as it happens' and for the capture of EVP-type audio anomalies. Unlike analogue cassettes, the recording quality is almost crystal clear. A MiniDisc recorder can be expensive but does eliminate the problem of limited memory space on a digital Dictaphone. However, be sure that you purchase a model that will take an external microphone, as some in the market do not. Also, don't forget spare batteries.

Mobile Phones

A mobile phone is ideal to keep with you in case of an emergency. We would always recommend that they are kept switched off during an investigation, as they can interfere with any type of equipment being used and may cause all your results to be inaccurate.

Motion Detectors

These devices are best suited for indoor investigations but are not very useful for outside investigations due to the effect from natural influences, such as wind, animals, etc. There are also top-of-the-range video cameras that can be activated through movement, thus saving you from watching hours of empty tape!

Night-Vision Camcorders

The majority of the newer camcorders will have some form of night vision. The extent of the night vision is measured in 'Lux' — and the lower it is the better. If you are buying a camcorder specifically for night-time recording, it's best to go for a 0 (zero) lux, which the majority of Sony camcorders have. Alternatively, you can purchase additional accessories that intensify the night-vision capabilities of your camcorder. Night vision can drain batteries very quickly so remember to take extra!

Night-Vision Scopes

This is ideal when you are investigating outside, as it will allow you to see what is making that unusual noise, without having to use a torch that will be seen by everyone. The scope intensifies all available light to give an image and often comes with magnifying properties as well.

Notebooks

A notebook is normally the most essential piece of equipment you can take with you. It is used to write down what takes place during an investigation, for example, temperature, smells, noises, the times these happen, who was in the room, etc. Don't forget to take plenty of pens or pencils!

Ouija Boards

This is a controversial piece of equipment and has been know to cause investigations to be cancelled once the owner of the property is aware that one may be used. Our recommendations is to make sure well ahead of time that the property owner has no issues with the use of a Ouija board. If they do have an issue with it, then don't use it or even take it with you.

Talcum Powders

This is used to determine whether there has been any interfering human of paranormal influences. Sprinkle it around on the ground or table around where the investigation is taking place. Remember that this does make a mess, so take something to clean it up afterwards!

Tape Recorders

It is not essential that a digital recorder be used to obtain EVP recordings. They can be recorded on any good tape recorder, but you will have more luck if you use an external static-free microphone. Remember to use tapes that are new or that have not been used before.

Thermometers

Most paranormal investigators prefer to use the trigger laser digital thermometers. However, they will only record the temperature of a solid object, such as a wall or piece of furniture. Therefore, any good thermometer can be used to detect changes in room temperature. Many will allow you to leave them in a room and record the maximum and minimum temperatures during that time period.

Torch

An essential piece of equipment since the majority of investigations take place during the night or in darkened rooms. It is advisable to take plenty of batteries with you — through experience, they always seem to be drained just when you need them the most! We prefer to use Maglite torches because they have a far more powerful beam than other torches of their size. LED torches are not always as bright but the batteries have fewer drainage issues.

Trigger Objects

Many people use old coins, a crucifix or children's toys. However, it is best to use an item that has been known to move in poltergeist activity or an item that has an association with the location. It is best to locate the item where it wouldn't normally be placed. It is also a good idea to 'lock off' a camcorder on the item to be able to prove whether the movement was caused by paranormal or human interference.

Tripods

These are a good idea when you want to 'lock off' a camcorder in a room. They are also used for taking still camera shots. There is always an issue with vibrations when it comes to cases involving movement, so try to make sure your tripod is on solid ground, not on tables or movable surfaces.

Walkie-Talkies or Two-Way Radios

Walkie-talkies are a good piece of equipment when investigating large or outdoor areas. They will allow you to keep in contact with the rest of the group and to report any activity that takes place. As with mobile phones, be aware that they can have an effect on any experiments that are taking place; this is especially important when, in the middle of something fantastic and paranormal happening, someone radios through to say they are ordering pizza.

Watches

Essential for recording the time that paranormal activity takes place. Many investigations are run to a time schedule, so it is essential to keep track of the time. We would recommend that you use a watch that has some type of illuminator to save on your torch batteries.

Sensory Mapping

This can be a valuable tool in the form of measurable statistical results. The idea behind it is to get everyone you can to wander around the entire area and note any feelings, emotions or sensory response they get.

When we do this, we break into groups of two and walk around the entire venue — one of us filming and the other just saying anything that they sense or feel. You may feel silly behaving in a Derek Acorah from *Most Haunted* fashion, almost as though you are a world-famous medium making your TV debut. Once the embarrassment factor has gone, you can replay the video and note down on a map of the building anything and everything you said. Ideally, you should mark on the map as you walk around but some people find this hard because they like to close their eyes to get more of a feel of a place.

We have been amazed by the results that this method has produced. For example, one venue we went to was a huge outdoor park, and the person walking around it had never been there before and knew nothing about the phenomena that had taken place. He walked around and said that he felt like he was being watched by something that was stood in the field next to the park, something from the Civil War period. About three hours later, someone else turned up and had a go at the same thing. He went straight to the same place as the previous man and said that he felt like there was a Cavalier looking at him. Now, the interesting thing was that neither person had been in the park before, and yet they both pointed to somewhere outside of the park, even though they both knew that the thing they were supposed to be investigating was within the park.

Now some people may think this is a foolish thing to do, as though we are claiming to be mediums. However, oddly, you will often get fantastic results from people who think that it is silly. It is a test that can be replicated over and over again and will only give you more and more information.

When you have plotted on the map the areas that things happen in or emotions are felt, then, if possible, use a computer program like Photoshop to scan and place the maps on top of each other. This way you will instantly be able to see the correlations if there are any. Failing the computer, the way I used to do this was to hold them up to the light and trace through them, proving you don't need money to do these experiments.

If this is done early on in the evening, it may give you a good idea where to place some locked-off cameras or microphones. If everyone is feeling a particular emotion in a certain place, it is a good idea to carefully examine the area to see if the architecture or decorations could have caused it, a low ceiling for example creating a sense of panic due to the sense of lack of space, or certain colours creating an emotional response, red for anger, blue for peace and so on.

We have managed to find in every venue that we have gone to correlations between the mapping process of individuals that seem to defy luck, and very often also correspond to the ghost stories of the venue, that is why it is very important to make sure the people doing this do not know the history of haunting within the building. Do not be afraid to write down anything, regardless of how stupid it sounds or feels, as someone else may write exactly the same thing, this doesn't prove that it is haunted but will show unusual occurrences.

It may not produce any evidence for a ghost but it may help rule out some psychological triggers for sightings; it can also make a very boring night of nothing happening actually reveal some statistical evidence of some worth.

Problems

One thing you need to remember is to try and keep whoever is doing it as uncontaminated as possible when it comes to information about the venue and the events that have ever taken place there. Once, in a room in a castle called the hanging room someone said they felt as though they couldn't breathe. Now, one obvious reason for this is that the person read the name on the door of the room and subconsciously invented a story about it in their head — which manifested itself as a choking sensation.

Base Readings

One of the most important things to do before you start getting spooked out at an investigation is to do the base tests. After acquiring a map of the area, make sure you have many photocopies of it. You will need several of these, as each one will be used to record different base test results.

Temperature

Ideally you want a thermometer that can log data, one that can be left somewhere for five minutes and will tell you the top and bottom temperatures during that period of time. You need to find the normal temperature of the rooms you are going into, ideally the night before as well as the night you are investigating, and hope that weather conditions will be similar on both nights. When you have a room temperature, you need to go around the room looking for heat sources, such as fires, heaters, light bulbs and so on. All of these heat sources need to be marked on the map. For example, if your average room temperature is about eighteen degrees but, when you walk across the room towards a window it drops, then this needs to be marked on the map.

Mark the time the temperature was taken as well as the date on the map — you can always check weather records for freak temperatures and conditions in that area.

EMF

There is a great deal of controversy over EMF meters and whether they actually do anything. For those of you who do not know what they are, they are devices that measure electromagnetic frequency.

The reason these may be important is that it is generally thought that ghosts give off a high level of electromagnetic fields or fluctuations. Now, as electrical devices give off varying levels of electromagnetic waves, a large number of electric appliances in the vicinity can ruin your results.

It's generally assumed that anything over 10 milligaus is a high reading and could possibly cause harm to your health, but also indicate a weird presence of paranormal activity. However, they often give false readings depending on which direction you point them in.

For this reason, when doing your base-line readings, you need to make a decision which direction to point the meter, and keep it that way throughout the entire mapping process. When we do them, we use the four main compass points and take readings of the entire place. These are then marked on the map, indicating any area of high readings and noting electrical appliances that may be causing them, such as heaters, microwaves and so forth.

Throughout the evening you should make readings and note these as well; keep the EMF meter to hand, as hopefully, if something occurs, you can check whether any interesting phenomena correspond to high readings.

One very useful thing to note is any electrics that may be in the walls, as wiring can give off readings as well. Hand-held metal detectors can be used for this purpose as well.

Draughts

A candle can be used to show if there are any draughts near windows and doors. We had a case where a woman thought that she had a presence in her house, indicated by a breeze through the house that seemed to circle around her when she sat in a chair; we managed to work out that this was due to a faulty loft hatch.

Noises

It is a good idea to indicate on the maps any noises that occur naturally, for example, if a room has a squeaky floorboard or the door has a faulty latch. These kind of things can prove invaluable and stop you wasting hours of time later on during the investigation.

Dust

If the room has a large amount of dust or other material, such as cobwebs, note this down as it may affect the photographs taken throughout the evening. This may seem trivial but it will save you, or the rest of your team, a great deal of effort when it comes to photograph analysis.

We did an investigation in an area that had a lot of building material and we seemed to capture more photos of orbs here than anywhere else — obviously, this was due to all the dust.

Audio

There are various ways of capturing audio, which basically break down into two groups: analogue and digital.

Analogue generally describes things recorded onto magnetic tapes, like a normal tape recorder or video recorder, and digital really refers to modern technology, like a MiniDisc recorder or MP3.

There are certain experiments to try and capture EVP, or electronic voice phenomena. They generally are conducted by either leaving a recording device in a room or venue and then listening back to see if there are any noises on it or by having the recording equipment there and asking questions of whatever entity you think may be there, leaving long enough gaps for it to be able to answer you.

Some people believe that analogue is actually better for recording phenomena, and there are great sections of the Internet devoted to EVP. I have yet to hear any that would really convince me of this system working, as most seem to have used filtering software to make it more audible or clear. The main issues surrounding this relates to how synthesisers work: if you take any sound and filter it and process it, you can make it sound like anything you want it to. So, avoid the temptation to clean up sounds. Leave them as they are when producing them as evidence.

Digital technology is easier to use. Sound, recorded onto memory cards or MP3 players, can be instantly downloaded, and this means the memory cards or whatever can be used again. This allows for hours of recording without breaking the bank trying to pay for more and more tapes.

Try to use a microphone that is on a stand and has some form of vibration protection. Perhaps place it on some foam to stop it recording noises that are actually vibrations through the floor or people kicking the microphone stand.

You may find that a lot of EVP practitioners will tell you that the sounds need to be filtered or listened to by people with an ear that is used to hearing them. However, when it comes to evidence, if you need to try and work out what is being said on a recording, then it isn't clear enough to be used as evidence for anything. Therefore, good EVP is hard to find, but it is fantastic when you do find it!

We recorded a few words being said in a pub that we were investigating, and because we had cameras in the room as well, we could go back and check that none of us made the noises we heard without resorting to ventriloquism, which I am pretty sure no one in that room was capable of.

It is always a good idea, if you have equipment to spare, to have a recording going at all times, as you can use it to cross-reference timings of events and also because it might be that you get results on the tape that were not audible to the people present or vice versa.

Thermometers

There are several different types of thermometer available on the market and it is a good idea to try and get as many types as you can, as they all function in varying ways.

The Traditional Mercury Thermometer
This is the type that everyone knows and it is a good indicator of room temperature or surface temperature, if placed on things like metal or stone. The good thing about this type of thermometer is that they are cheap and you can actually see a physical response to temperature change.

Digital Thermometers
We often use a thermometer that has two temperature gauges, one on the main body of the instrument and one on a long wire attached to it. This is so that you can use it indoors and place the wire outside the window to give indoor and outdoor temperatures. It is also very useful for measuring the temperature in two different parts of the room.

Laser Thermometers
These come in varying levels of quality and can give very different results depending on their capability. You fire a laser thermometer at a surface, like a wall, and it bounces back the temperature to you. These are extremely useful when you need to know instant temperature readings at a place that is some distance from you. Please read their instructions very carefully, as they can vary in ability greatly, normally depending on cost. Also, the further away from an object, the greater the area of temperature the thermometer is trying to read, because the beam gets wider.

Thermometer Problems
The biggest problem you will find is that you may have two thermometers in the same place but showing two different temperatures. This is often due to the fact that they are not calibrated correctly, but do not worry too much about this, as any one instrument will be accurate with itself; if one thermometer goes up by two degrees then others should as well.

We had a very interesting case where three thermometers in the same place showed temperatures rising and falling between seven and twenty-one degrees over a period of five minutes. They were all showing different temperatures even though placed next to each other. The important thing is that any one of those instruments showed a measurable phenomena, even though they differed from each other

Trigger Objects

Trigger objects is the general term that encompasses the idea of trying to get a ghost or spirit to physically move something. There are many types of trigger object experiment, and this can be one of the cheapest experiments to do — and one of the most spectacular if you get any response.

A common trigger experiment is to place a coin on a plate and then lightly cover it in a thin layer of flour, this is done so that, if someone pushes the coin, their fingerprints will be visible, and also the coin moving will displace the flour and show you how far it moved and what path it took.

An even more simple experiment is to place an object onto a piece of paper and draw around it; if the item moves, then obviously the outline will no longer be around the object. If you have enough cameras to spare, then lock one off just focused on this; make sure the entire item is in frame, otherwise you cannot guarantee that it wasn't moved off screen.

It can be a good idea, if you can get permission from the building owner, to draw around furniture with chalk, so if you do get the rare occurrence of furniture movement, then it will show up straight away.

Some people think it is a good idea to use an item that in some way corresponds to the haunting. If it is generally presumed to be a small child that haunts the place, then use toys or try and find an object that dates from the time of the original ghost. Obviously, this is difficult, as you are second guessing when the ghost once lived.

We use a very interesting system for trigger objects: a poltergeist box. A box was made using clear Perspex, that could be placed over the experiment; this box is then alarmed, so that if it is lifted, the alarms go off. This means that it can be left in a room with no fear of anyone interfering with it.

Make sure that, once the item is placed, you photograph it from all angles, as when you return to the item, you may think that it has moved a few millimetres but, on examining the photographs, realise it hasn't.

Problems

The main problem you will face with this experiment is vibration. In old buildings, floorboards can cause something to move at the other end of a room, so on your base tests, try and see if there are any natural vibrations in the room, possibly caused by traffic outside or people walking inside.

Draughts may also cause you problems, as it could cause the flour or talc to be blown around, and make sure you use an item with a small amount of weight to it for the same reason. Obviously, objects like marbles are going to have their own problems if not on a completely flat, solid surface.

Incident Report Forms

These are the forms we use to investigate a haunting; sometimes people do not wish to fill these in, which is fair enough — you cannot force people to answer questions. An example of an incident report form is below.

Please answer as many questions as you feel you can. Also please indicate whether you mind this information becoming public knowledge. Anything you wish to be kept secret (such as names and addresses, etc.) please put a P with a ring around it at the end of the line. If all of the information given is to be kept private then please write that at the top of each page.

01. Name
02. Contact number
03. Address
04. Email
05. Please write the most detailed description you can of the event; you will probably need another piece of paper for this, or use the rear of this one; please number the sheets you use 1 of 3, 2 of 3, etc., depending on how many you use.
06. The location of the event (full address) and location within that address, (which room, etc.)
07. Date of experience
08. Time of experience
09. Weather conditions
10. People present (if people do not wish to put their names down then just the number of people present)
11. People present who witnessed or shared the experience
12. People present who experienced nothing (in case it was central to just one person or one group)
13. Has this ever happened before, if so, has anyone else witnessed it?
14. If this was a sighting, did it appear to be solid and lifelike, or did it appear in some other form? Please describe to the best of your ability.
15. If this was a noise, then please describe to the best of your ability what it sounded like, or any other interesting elements to the noise.
16. Were you expecting anything unusual to occur, for example, were you at a haunted castle, playing with Ouija boards, watching horror films etc.?
17. Did you have an interest in the paranormal before this event?
18. Have you experienced any notable paranormal events in your life before?
19. Did the experience remind you of anyone or anything that has happened before?
20. Did you react to each other, as though there was an intelligence behind it? Did it speak to you or answer you or move as though it saw you? Did its behaviour indicate that it had acknowledged your existence?
21. How did you feel? Any emotional response from you should be noted, however strange it sounds.

22. Were there any other unusual occurrences before, during or after the event? This may be in the form of noises, sounds, smells or even lack of them.
23. Were you tired or even asleep when it occurred?
24. Can you explain your state of mind at the time? e.g. were you stressed, tired, upset, happy, etc.?
25. How did you feel before it happened?
26. How did you feel as it was happening?
27. How did you feel afterwards?
28. Does the location have any previous history of strange experiences that you knew of?
29. Were you on any form of medication at all? Please name any medication if you can.
30. Were you on any form of recreational drug, including alcohol, during the previous two days?
31. Do you have any form of hearing or sight problems?
32. Has the experience made you feel any different since it occurred, for example, a belief in God or an afterlife? Has it, for example, made you feel happier or more depressed?
34. Is there anything of interest that you can think of that you feel you should tell us about the event or yourself?

At the end of the last sentence, please date and sign the page and write how many pages in total your report has come to, especially if you have written on extra pieces of paper.

CONCLUSION

So, in conclusion, do you believe in ghosts now? I hope not in some ways; I think that if you have read my book and now suddenly believe in ghosts, then you are far too easily led. The point about being a ghost hunter is to try and work out for yourself what is going on. Over all the years I have been doing this, I have never taken anything for granted. I have always questioned what I am told and I hope you will do the same.

The worst thing that can happen to you when you set out on your ghost-hunting quest is that you will meet a large contingency of ghost hunters who claim they have all the answers — they don't. The only people worth listening to are the ones who tell you they don't know what something is, but then go on to tell you that there are theories that it may be x, y or z.

Please do not part with any hard-earned, or even not particularly hard-earned cash, for mediums, psychics and paranormal predators. There are a few good ones out there but a much larger percentage of awful ones; there are many people waiting to take your money. I have heard tales of groups that charge you money to come and investigate your ghosts, and groups that charge over £100 for you to join them for a few hours on an investigation. Stay away from these people, for where there are large amounts of money involved, there are high expectations, and very high expectations lead to fraud. Paying £5 for a ghost walk, or even £50 to stay in a haunted hotel is not extortionate, but when you find yourself paying twice the price to stay somewhere just because a medium will be present, then you need to start asking some serious questions.

The best thing about ghost hunting is that it is free. I have included some outdoor venues that are reliably reported as haunted, so start there with just a pen and paper. More importantly, if you get any good results then send them to me. Share your experiences with other groups, as they may have investigated that area as well. The more information we have about haunted places the better, as we can either disprove or prove the existence of the resident ghosts with facts, figures, recordings and data. Good luck out there!

Go to www.parasoc.org to read investigation papers and report any more Cheltenham ghosts. You may even end up featuring in my next book — who knows?

FURTHER READING

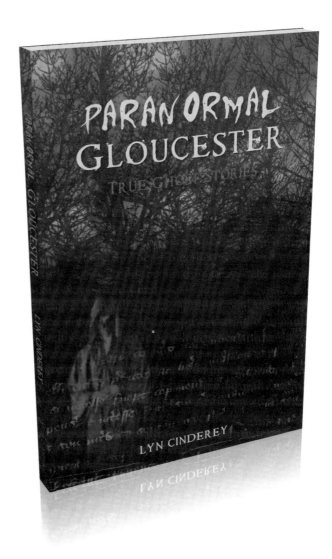

Paranormal Gloucester
Lyn Cinderey

ISBN 978-1-84868-249-8
£12.99

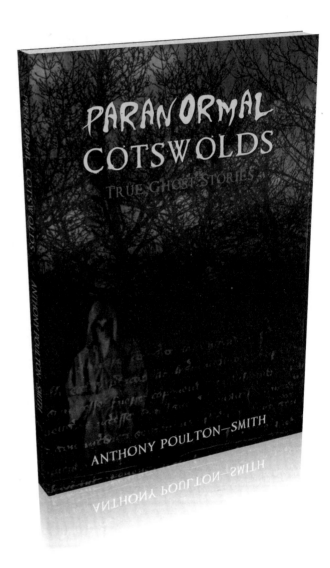

Paranormal Cotswolds
Anthony Poulton-Smith

ISBN 978-1-84868-170-5
£12.99

Available from all good bookshops or order direct from
our website www.amberleybooks.com